C. Hart

Asterix Omnibus

ASTERIX AND THE ACTRESS, ASTERIX AND THE CLASS ACT, ASTERIX AND THE FALLING SKY

Written and illustrated by ALBERT UDERZO

Exclusive licensee: Orion Publishing Group
Translators: Anthea Bell and Derek Hockridge
Typography: Bryony Newhouse

Asterix and The Actress
Original title: *Astérix et Latraviata*

Inking: Frédéric Mébarki
Colour work: Thierry Mébarki
Co-ordination: Studio 'Et Cetera'

Asterix and the Class Act
Original title: *Astérix et la Rentrée Gauloise*

Co-ordination: Studio 'Et Cetera'

Asterix and the Falling Sky
Original title: Le Ciel Lui Tombe Sur La Tête

Inking: Frédéric Mébarki
Colour work: Thierry Mébarki
Co-ordination: Studio 56

This edition first published in Great Britain in 2007 by
Orion Books Ltd,
Orion House, 5 Upper St Martin's Lane
London WC2H 9EA
An Hachette Livre UK Company

Printed in Italy

http://gb.asterix.com
www.orionbooks.co.uk

A CIP catalogue record for this book is available from the British Library

ISBN 978 0 7528 9156 9 (Hardback)
ISBN 978 0 7528 9158 3 (Export Paperback)

The Orion Publishing Group's policy is to use papers that are natural, renewable and recyclable and made from wood grown in sustainable forests. The logging and manufacturing processes are expected to conform to the environmental regulations of the country of origin.

THE YEAR IS 50 BC. GAUL IS ENTIRELY OCCUPIED BY THE ROMANS. WELL, NOT ENTIRELY ... ONE SMALL VILLAGE OF INDOMITABLE GAULS STILL HOLDS OUT AGAINST THE INVADERS. AND LIFE IS NOT EASY FOR THE ROMAN LEGIONARIES WHO GARRISON THE FORTIFIED CAMPS OF TOTORUM, AQUARIUM, LAUDANUM AND COMPENDIUM ...

ASTERIX, THE HERO OF THESE ADVENTURES. A SHREWD, CUNNING LITTLE WARRIOR, ALL PERILOUS MISSIONS ARE IMMEDIATELY ENTRUSTED TO HIM. ASTERIX GETS HIS SUPERHUMAN STRENGTH FROM THE MAGIC POTION BREWED BY THE DRUID GETAFIX . . .

OBELIX, ASTERIX'S INSEPARABLE FRIEND. A MENHIR DELIVERY MAN BY TRADE, ADDICTED TO WILD BOAR. OBELIX IS ALWAYS READY TO DROP EVERYTHING AND GO OFF ON A NEW ADVENTURE WITH ASTERIX – SO LONG AS THERE'S WILD BOAR TO EAT, AND PLENTY OF FIGHTING. HIS CONSTANT COMPANION IS DOGMATIX, THE ONLY KNOWN CANINE ECOLOGIST, WHO HOWLS WITH DESPAIR WHEN A TREE IS CUT DOWN.

GETAFIX, THE VENERABLE VILLAGE DRUID, GATHERS MISTLETOE AND BREWS MAGIC POTIONS. HIS SPECIALITY IS THE POTION WHICH GIVES THE DRINKER SUPERHUMAN STRENGTH. BUT GETAFIX ALSO HAS OTHER RECIPES UP HIS SLEEVE . . .

CACOFONIX, THE BARD. OPINION IS DIVIDED AS TO HIS MUSICAL GIFTS. CACOFONIX THINKS HE'S A GENIUS. EVERYONE ELSE THINKS HE'S UNSPEAKABLE. BUT SO LONG AS HE DOESN'T SPEAK, LET ALONE SING, EVERYBODY LIKES HIM . . .

FINALLY, VITALSTATISTIX, THE CHIEF OF THE TRIBE. MAJESTIC, BRAVE AND HOT-TEMPERED, THE OLD WARRIOR IS RESPECTED BY HIS MEN AND FEARED BY HIS ENEMIES. VITALSTATISTIX HIMSELF HAS ONLY ONE FEAR, HE IS AFRAID THE SKY MAY FALL ON HIS HEAD TOMORROW. BUT AS HE ALWAYS SAYS, TOMORROW NEVER COMES.

R. GOSCINNY **Asterix** A. UDERZO

GOSCINNY AND UDERZO

PRESENT

An Asterix Adventure

ASTERIX AND THE ACTRESS

Written and Illustrated by ALBERT UDERZO

Translated by ANTHEA BELL *and* DEREK HOCKRIDGE

à Hugo
mon petit-fils

THE...THE VILLAGE IS DESERTED!

?!

HAPPY BIRTHDAY TO YOU, HAPPY BIRTHDAY TO YOU...!

I FORGOT IT WAS OUR BIRTHDAY TODAY!
THAT'S RIGHT... THE TWO OF YOU WERE BORN ON THE SAME DAY!

YES, BUT I GOT IN FIRST BY A FEW MINUTES! I CARRIED MORE WEIGHT!
HA!HA! HA!HA!

AND TO CELEBRATE THE OCCASION WE HAVE A LITTLE SURPRISE FOR YOU!

OOH, I CAN GUESS WHAT IT IS ... HEE! HEE! HEE!
OH YES? SO WHAT DO YOU THINK IT IS?

A WHOLE ROMAN LEGION JUST FOR THE TWO OF US!

TAP!
HMPH!

NO, NO, OBELIX! EVEN BETTER THAN THAT!
AARRGH!

MUMMY!
WOOF!

YOU CAME FROM CONDATUM* SPECIALLY FOR MY BIRTHDAY?
YES, YOU LITTLE RASCAL... SINCE YOU DON'T VISIT YOUR MUM, YOUR MUM HAS TO VISIT YOU!
?
*RENNES

MY LITTLE MUMMY! STILL AS LIGHT AS A FEATHER!
AND YOU'RE AS STRONG AS EVER, ICKLE OBELIXIKINS!
?

A GREAT BIRTHDAY BANQUET IS HELD IN THE GAULISH VILLAGE.
HOW DID YOU GET HERE? IT MUST HAVE BEEN A TIRING JOURNEY.
NOT SO MUCH TIRING AS INCONVENIENT!
SCRUNCH!! SCRUNCH!! SCRUNCH!!
3A

YES, WE WERE OFFERED CUT-PRICE TICKETS ON A LUTETIAN DELIVERY CART CARRYING FISH FOR UNHYGIENIX! THEY WERE GOING FOR A PONG!

SO LUCKILY WE SOON HITCHED A LIFT ON AN HGV!
WHAT'S AN HGV?

A HEAVY GAULISH VEHICLE, ICKLE OBELIXIKINS!

AND JUST HOW HEAVY DO YOU THINK THIS GAULISH FIST IS?

WHY DIDN'T OUR DADS COME WITH YOU?

THEY'LL BE JOINING US LATER. THEIR ARMORICAN SOUVENIR BUSINESS IS IN FULL SWING JUST NOW.
YES, THIS IS THE MIDDLE OF THE CONDATUM TOURIST SEASON.
3B

OH, AND YOUR DAD SAYS HE'S SORRY HE CAN'T BE WITH US, AND HE'S SENT YOU THIS SWORD AS A PRESENT!
!?

JUST WHAT I WANTED! JUDGING BY THE PRECIOUS STONES ON ITS SHEATH, IT MUST HAVE BELONGED TO SOME RICH ROMAN OFFICER!

ACTUALLY IT BELONGED TO A DRUNK... A FORMER LEGIONARY. HE SWAPPED IT WITH US FOR A BARREL OF BARLEY BEER!
SMACK!
SCRUNCH! SCRUNCH!

HE LEFT US THIS HELMET TOO. YOU CAN ADD IT TO YOUR COLLECTION, OBELIXIWIXIKINS!
!
PFFFFFFFF

ANYBODY WANT TO TRY THIS HELMET ON? IF SO I'M READY TO JAM IT ON HIS HEAD, HARD! THAT'LL TEACH HIM TO TRY THINGS ON WITH ME!
4A

MEANWHILE, IN CONDATUM...
MODERNITIES & COLLECTABLES

GAULISH POTTERY IS AN EXCELLENT INVESTMENT, BOUND TO APPRECIATE IN VALUE. IT'S GOT A GREAT FUTURE AHEAD OF IT!
WE HAVE MENHIRS IN ALL SIZES AVAILABLE, HAND-CRAFTED, SIGNED, CARVED FROM PURE ARMORICAN GRANITE!
OBELIX

ROLL UP, FOLKS, ROLL UP! WHO DOESN'T HAVE A DOLMEN YET? EASY SELF-ASSEMBLY!
UNUSED HELMET
SLIGHTLY USED HELMET
4B

LATER...
A GOOD DAY'S SALES! WE DID WELL TO STAY ON IN CONDATUM FOR A BIT, OBELISCOIDIX!
YOU'RE RIGHT, ASTRONOMIX! AND NO REASON WHY WE SHOULDN'T HAVE A BIRTHDAY PARTY WITH OUR LADS LATER!

HOW ABOUT CRACKING OPEN A BARREL OF BARLEY BEER?
GOOD IDEA... WITH A COUPLE OF CRACKING GOOD ROAST WILD BOAR TOO!

YOU STUPID OLD SOAK! YOU MEAN YOU RECOGNISE THEM? THAT'S THEM?
LOOK... HIC! I KEEP TELLING YOU... HIC, HAEC, HOC!... IT'S THEM! YOU MUSHT BE AS DRUNK AS A SHKUNK... I MEAN DEAF AS A POSHT!

BACK IN THE VILLAGE.
NO ONE'S DONE ANY HOUSE-WORK AROUND THIS HUT IN DONKEY'S YEARS! NOW LISTEN, ASTERIX, SON, WHEN ARE YOU GOING TO FIND A NICE WIFE?
UM... ER... OH, MUM, I DON'T SEE WHY I'D WANT A WIFE!!

STUFF AND NONSENSE! YOU DON'T LOOK WELL EITHER! TIME YOU STOPPED LEADING THIS WILD LIFE, MY BOY!

OBELIXIKINS! YOOHOO! DINNER'S READY!
COMING, COMING! MMM! YUM, YUM!

YOUR DIET ISN'T VARIED ENOUGH, SO I'VE MADE YOU SOME GOOD NOURISHING SOUP TO GIVE YOU A LITTLE SURPRISE!
?!

PROBABLY NOT A NICE ONE EITHER!

WELL, OBELIXIKINS, WHEN ARE YOU GOING TO GET YOURSELF A NICE WIFE TO COOK YOU HEALTHY WELL-BALANCED MEALS?
SPLUTTER! SPLUTTER! SPLUTTER!

AND IN CONDATUM...
A BRIGHT IDEA SHETTING UP BUSINESH IN CONDATUM, DON'T YOU... THINK, HIC!... OBELISCOIDIX?
YUP... AND YOU GET SHOMETHING A BIT STRONGER THAN GOAT'SH MILK HERE... HEE! HEE!

MIND YOU, I SHOMETIMESH MISS THE VILLAGE OF OUR CHILDHOOD... HIC!
THAT'SH RIGHT ... HIC! ... THE VILLAGE OF OUR YOUTH...

IT'S WHERE OUR LADS LIVE TOO... HIC!
OH, DON'T, OBIE! JUST THINKING OF IT MAKES ME ALL WEEPY... HIC!

?!?!

BY TOUTATIS!!! WE'VE BEEN BURGLED!
MODERN

THEY'VE TURNED THE PLACE OVER, BUT I DON'T SEE ANYTHING MISSING!
THAT'S ODD. MAYBE THEY WERE AFTER SOMETHING SPECIAL.

DEAD RIGHT! AND WE DIDN'T FIND IT!
?!

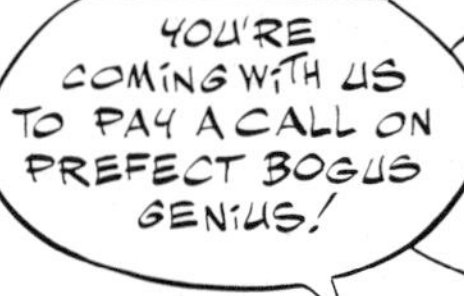
YOU'RE COMING WITH US TO PAY A CALL ON PREFECT BOGUS GENIUS!

IT'S LUCKY FOR YOU WE'RE A COUPLE OF OLD WRECKS NOWADAYS, LITTLE TITCH!

BUT JUST YOU WAIT TILL OUR SONS HEAR ABOUT THIS!
EVER BEEN HIT ON THE HEAD WITH A MENHIR BEFORE?

AVE, PREFECT BOGUS GENIUS! THESE ARE THE MEN SUSPECTED OF DOING THE DEAL WITH THE DEFENDANT.

RECOGNISE THEM, TREMENSDELIRIUS?
HIC!... YESH, YOU BET ...HAEC! HOC!
SCRATCH! SCRATCH! SCRATCH!

AS A SOLDIER WHO HAS SERVED IN THE LEGIONS* AREN'T YOU ASHAMED OF ABUSING YOUR COMMANDER'S TRUST?
WELL, YEAH ... BUT... HIC! ... I WAS THIRSHTY!
* SEE "ASTERIX AND CAESAR'S GIFT"

PUT THIS WINESKIN IN A DEEP, DARK CELLAR. MAYBE HE'LL IMPROVE WITH A LITTLE TIME IN THE COOLER!
THAT WINO HAS BEEN FOUND GUILTY OF STEALING A SWORD AND A HELMET, THE PROPERTY OF A VERY HIGH-RANKING ROMAN DIGNITARY! CAN YOU TWO TELL ME WHERE THOSE ARMS ARE?
7A

YOU BET WE CAN...

IN THE HANDS OF OUR SONS ASTERIX AND OBELIX!!!
AND YOU'LL SEE A THING OR TWO WHEN THEY TURN UP! YOU JUST WAIT!!!
IT'S A LITTLE QUIRK OF THEIRS... THEY'RE ALWAYS QUOTING FROM THAT PLAY WAITING FOR GODOTRIX

OH NO! I NEVER EXPECTED TO FIND THAT THE SWORD AND HELMET HAD FALLEN INTO THE HANDS OF THOSE TWO FEROCIOUS GAULS!!!

BACK IN THE HOMES OF THE FEROCIOUS GAULS, LIFE IS PASSING PEACEFULLY BY... ALTHOUGH AT TIMES...
STOP WAVING YOUR ARMS ABOUT, ASTERIX, OR I'LL NEVER GET YOUR HAIR WASHED!
BUT MUM, THERE'S SOAP IN MY EYES!
7B

I'VE INVITED SOME OF THE NEIGHBOURING YOUNG LADIES AND THEIR DAUGHTERS TO TAKE A CUP OF GOAT'S MILK, SO DO TRY TO BE POLITE TO THEM, RIXIKINS!

GOOD AFTERNOON, MA'AM! MY SON AND I ARE SO PLEASED TO SEE YOU!

HOW ARE YOU? YOU KNOW MY SON ALREADY, OF COURSE! DO COME IN, EVERYONE!

OH! WHAT A GRACEFUL GIRL YOUR DAUGHTER IS!

SIGH!
WELL, WELL... HERE'S SOMEONE WHO MUST SET PLENTY OF HEARTS BEATING!

I DON'T SAY SO BECAUSE SHE'S MY DAUGHTER, BUT...
AS FOR MY LITTLE GIRL, YOU WOULDN'T BELIEVE HOW TALENTED SHE IS!
OH, YOU REALLY OUGHT TO TASTE MY DAUGHTER'S COOKING...
BY THE WAY, JUST HOW OLD IS YOUR SON?
I HAVE TO CONFESS THAT QUALITIES SUCH AS MY CHILD'S ARE RARE!...

... AND SO ON AND SO FORT
... AND ON AN AND
ENOUGH!!!
... AND SO ON AND SO FORTH AND ...
AND SO FORTH...
... AND SO ON AND SO FORTH
AND AND SO FORTH

WHY... WHAT IS IT, RIXIKINS?
NO!! I'M NOT READY FOR THE RESPONSIBILITY OF MARRIAGE YET!!!
POC!

HONESTLY! I ASK YOU!!!

!

OH NO!! NOT YOU TOO!

HA!HA!HA!
HEE!HEE!
HO!HO!HO!HO!
?

WELL, A BIT OF A LAUGH DOES YOU GOOD!
YOU'RE RIGHT, BUT I CAN'T DENY I'D BE GLAD TO SEE OUR FATHERS TURN UP SOON.

BUT IN THE PRISON OF THE PREFECTURE IN CONDATUM...
TREMENSDELIRIUS, WHO DID THAT SWORD AND HELMET BELONG TO?
POMPEY, THE CONSUL EXPELLED FROM THE ROMAN SENATE BY JULIUS CAESAR... OH, I'VE GOT A TERRIBLE THIRST!...

SO WHAT'S HE DOING IN GAUL?
I HEARD HE'S TRYING TO RAISE AN ARMY AGAINST HIS GREAT ENEMY CAESAR ... I'M JUST DYING FOR A DRINK!

WELL? SO WHAT KEEPS YOU FROM RECOVERING THAT SO-AND-SO HELMET AND THAT SO-AND-SO SWORD, BOGUS GENIUS?
O GREAT POMPEY, NO ONE CAN APPROACH THE VILLAGE OF THOSE INVINCIBLE GAULS. IT'S SURROUNDED BY CAESAR'S GARRISONS!
YOU'VE GOT A POINT! IF CAESAR HAD EVIDENCE OF MY PRESENCE IN GAUL, OUR PLANS WOULD BE SCUPPERED!
WE MUST ACT WITH CUNNING AND THE UTMOST DISCRETION! I THINK I HAVE THE ANSWER, O NOBLE POMPEY!

LATER, IN THE VILLAGE...
RIGHT! VANILLA AND I HAVE DECIDED TO HAVE A REAL BIRTHDAY PARTY FOR YOU TWO!
BUT...

...BUT WE'VE ALREADY HAD A BIRTHDAY BANQUET FOR THE WHOLE VILLAGE!

IF YOU ASK ME, THAT WAS JUST AN EXCUSE FOR THE USUAL BINGE!
I LIKE A BINGE EVEN WHEN IT ISN'T MY BIRTHDAY!

WELL THIS TIME WE'RE GOING TO INVITE ALL THE BARDS FROM THE SURROUNDING VILLAGES TO PLAY MUSIC SO THAT THE YOUNG PEOPLE OF OUR OWN VILLAGE CAN DANCE!
INCLUDING YOU TWO, OF COURSE!

MEANWHILE, YOU CAN MAKE YOURSELVES USEFUL...
...BY PICKING SOME PRETTY FLOWERS TO DECORATE THE VILLAGE!
10A

I STILL SAY THERE'S NOTHING I LIKE BETTER THAN A BANQUET ON MY BIRTHDAY!
YES, AND I BET I KNOW TWO PEOPLE ENJOYING PLENTY OF BANQUETS!!!
Fishmonger UNHYGIENIX

BY BELENOS! WHAT ARE OUR BOYS WAITING FOR? WHY DON'T THEY COME TO THE RESCUE?
THEY'D HAVE TO KNOW WHERE WE ARE FIRST!

WELL, BOGUS GENIUS, SO WHAT'S THIS SOLUTION OF YOURS?

?
HERE IT IS!!
10B

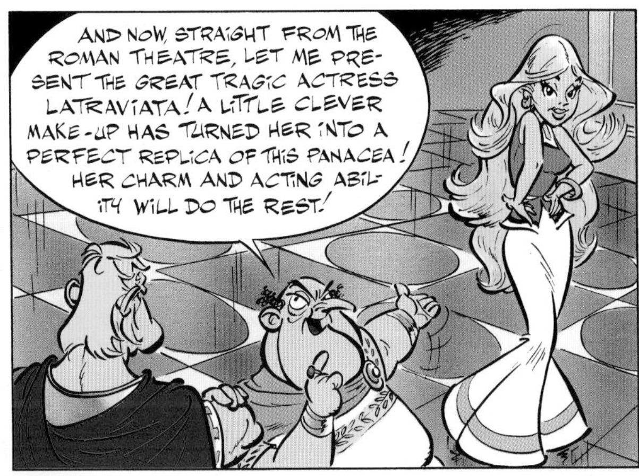

LOOK AT THOSE TWO GREAT GOOFS! CAN'T EVEN SUMMON UP THE COURAGE TO ASK A GIRL TO DANCE!

AFTER WE WENT TO ALL THAT TROUBLE, TOO!

11B

WANT TO DANTHE, ATHTERICTH?
I'M SO SORRY, BUT I'M A TERRIBLE DANCER! NOW OBELIX HERE IS TERRIFIC!
?!

COME ON THEN OBELICTH, SHALL WE DANTHE?
OOH, I D-D-DAREN'T!
GO ON, OBELIX, DON'T BE SO SILLY!

12A

CLAP! CLAP! CLAP! CLAP! CLAP! CLAP! CLAP! CLAP! CLAP!

HE'S GOT RHYTHM, MY OBELIXIKINS! SEE HIM DANCE THE POLKA!
MORE OF A BELLY DANCE, IF YOU ASK ME. YOUR LITTLE OBELIXIKINS WON'T FIND MANY PARTNERS AT THIS RATE!

WHAT A SHAME! WHILE THEY WERE PLAYING MUSIC THEY WEREN'T THINKING OF PLAYING ABOUT WITH US!
I NEVER APPRECIATED CELTIC MUSIC SO MUCH IN MY LIFE!
12B

RIGHT, LATRAVIATA, REMEMBER YOU WERE WANDERING ABOUT! YOU'VE LOST YOUR MEMORY, AND CAN'T RECALL ANYTHING EXCEPT THE NAME OF OBELIX!
DON'T YOU WORRY, FASTANDFURIUS. THIS WILL BE AN EASY ROLE FOR AN ACTRESS OF MY STATURE!

HALT! WHO ARE YOU AND WHERE ARE YOU GOING, ROMAN?
?!

FASTANDFURIUS AT YOUR SERVICE, LEGIONARY! I'M A MERCHANT TRADING IN THE GAULISH COUNTRYSIDE.
AND WHO'S THIS PRETTY YOUNG GAULISH GIRL?

SHE'S ASKED ME TO TAKE HER TO HER NATIVE VILLAGE!
SO WHAT VILLAGE WOULD THAT BE?

THE PLACE WHERE A MAN CALLED OBELIX LIVES.
13A

EEK!... RIGHT! PASS, MERCHANT, AND YOU NEVER SET EYES ON US!
?

!

I WONDER IF IT WAS WISE OF ME TO ACCEPT THIS MISSION!
YOU LOOK VERY PREOCCUPIED, FASTANDFURIUS?!

I HOPE THEY RECOGNISE YOU LATRA ... I MEAN PANACEA!
IT'S MY TALENT THEY WILL RECOGNISE!
13B

GOOD GRIEF... IT'S PANACEA! WHAT ARE YOU DOING HERE?
PHEW!

THIS POOR GIRL IS SUFFERING FROM AMNESIA. SHE CAN'T REMEMBER ANYTHING!
BY TOUTATIS! I'LL TELL CHIEF VITALSTATISTIX!

IT WORKS! WELL DONE! YOU REALLY ARE A GREAT ACTRESS!
THAT'S NOT IT! I'M HORRIFIED AT THE IDEA OF STAYING IN A DUMP LIKE THIS!

SO THE NAME OF OBELIX LED YOU TO BRING PANACEA HERE?
YES! ON HEARING IT EVERYONE TOLD ME THE WAY TO YOUR VILLAGE!

ODD THAT THE POOR CHILD REMEMBERS OBELIX, BUT NOT HER HUSBAND TRAGICOMIX...?
14A

GO AND FIND OBELIX! PERHAPS THE SIGHT OF HIM WILL RESTORE HER FAILING MEMORY!

OBELIX, COME QUICK!! IT'S PANACEA! SHE WANTS TO SEE YOU!!!
!
?

PAN... PANACEA... PANACEA...
WELL, WHAT ARE YOU WAITING FOR, YOU GOOF?

ASTERIX! ASTERIX! PANACEA IS HERE AND SHE WANTS TO SEE ME! SHE REALLY DOES!!!
?!

EITHER OBELIX HAS LOST HIS WITS OR THERE'S SOMETHING FUNNY GOING ON!
OBELIX ALWAYS DID TAKE THINGS TO HEART, POOR BOY... AND HIS HEART'S EVEN BIGGER THAN HIS STOMACH!
14B

PANACEA HAS LOST HER MEMORY, BUT ODDLY ENOUGH SHE SEEMS TO REMEMBER YOUR NAME, OBELIX!
?!

OH! OBELIX!
WOO-ER!
GRRRRR!

I'M SO GLAD TO SEE YOU AGAIN, OBELIX!
WKRSFTSSS!

WHY HAVE YOU COME BACK TO THE VILLAGE, PANACEA, AND WHERE'S TRAGICOMIX?
?

WHO IS THIS LITTLE MAN?
WHY, ASTERIX, OF COURSE! MY BEST FRIEND ASTERIX!
?!
HUH!
15A

YOU MUST MAKE ALLOWANCES, ASTERIX! SHE REMEMBERS **ME**, BUT NO ONE ELSE!

OH, OF COURSE, ASTERIX! LET ME GIVE YOU A GREAT BIG HUG!
!

HM... I FEAR SHE MAY BE OVERDOING IT A BIT!

THE POOR CHILD MUST HAVE HAD SOME KIND OF TERRIBLE SHOCK. I'LL TAKE HER TO SEE HER FATHER SOPORIFIX TO RECOVER!
?????
?????
AS A TOKEN OF GRATITUDE, ROMAN, WE OFFER YOU OUR FAMOUS GAULISH HOSPITALITY!
AVE, CHIEF!

ER... THANKS CHIEF!
?!
15B

I HAVE A NASTY FEELING WE'RE GOING TO END OUR DAYS HERE IN JUG, OBELISCOIDIX!
AND I BET EVERYONE THINKS WE'RE OUT ON THE TILES WITH A BARREL OF BARLEY BEER!
SHUT UP ABOUT JUGS AND BARRELS, WILL YOU!

DON'T YOU WORRY, YOU OLD SOAK! IN HIS CLEMENCY, THE PREFECT HAS DECIDED TO SET YOU FREE TOMORROW!
!

OH! THANK YOU! THE BLESSINGS OF BACCHUS ON THE MAGNANIMOUS BOGUS GENIUS! MAY HIS CUP ALWAYS RUN OVER!
YOU'RE GETTING OFF LIGHTLY, TREMENSDELIRIUS...

...YOU'VE ONLY GOT TO TWO DO PUNISHMENT FATIGUES STOCKING UP THE WATER SUPPLY!

MERCY! NO! NOT THAT! I CAN'T STAND CONTACT WITH WATER!!!
SO WE GUESSED!
16A

THOSE BLIGHTERS WANT TO POISON ME!
WE HAVE A PROPOSITION TO PUT TO YOU, ROMAN!

WE GUESS YOU'LL BE ABLE TO LEAVE THE PREFECTURE BETWEEN YOUR TWO PUNISHMENT FATIGUES, RIGHT?
YEAH ... SO WHAT?

THIS PURSE FULL OF SESTERTII IS YOURS IF YOU PROMISE TO TELL OUR FRIENDS PANACEA AND TRAGICOMIX WHERE WE ARE! THEY LIVE IN THIS CITY!

YES, YES! I'LL DO IT! PANACEA AND TRAGICOMIX! IT'S A DEAL!

SOMEONE OUGHT TO GO AND SEE TRAGICOMIX IN CONDATUM! IT COULD BE URGENT!
OBELIX AND I WILL GO, GETAFIX! WE CAN CALL AND SEE OUR FATHERS TOO!
SUPPOSE I WAS TO SING JUST A TEENY-TINY POETIC ODE TO PANACEA...
16B

I HEAR YOU HAVE A FINE COLLECTION OF ROMAN HELMETS, OBELIX! CAN I SEE IT?
GRRRR!

IT'S AMAZING, OBELIX!
OH, WELL... ER... DO YOU REALLY THINK SS...?
HUH!

THIS IS THE ONE I LIKE BEST! I'M SURE THE MERCHANT FASTANDFURIUS WOULD BE WILLING TO BUY IT FROM YOU!
IT'S NOT FOR SALE...

IT'S A BIRTH-DAY PRESENT FROM HIS FATHER, YOUNG WOMAN!!!

OH, DO FORGIVE ME! I ONLY SUG-GESTED IT BECAUSE OF FASTAND-FURIUS ... HE'S BEEN SO KIND TO ME! IT WOULD HAVE BEEN A NICE WAY TO SAY THANK YOU!
17A

HERE! IT... IT'S YOURS NOW, PPPP...
?!

OH! THANK YOU! YOU'RE SUCH A SWEETIE, OBELIX!

WELL, I SUPPOSE YOU'RE FREE TO DO AS YOU SEE FIT WITH YOUR PRESENTS, OBELIX!

I DON'T KNOW ABOUT YOU SARSA-PARILLA, BUT I DON'T THINK MUCH OF THAT GIRL PANACEA!
I ENTIRELY AGREE! AMNESIA HAS NOT IMPROVED HER!

GOOD, HERE YOU ARE OBELIX! WE'RE OFF TO CONDATUM TO FIND TRAGICOMIX!
!
17B

OH, PLEASE, PLEASE DON'T LEAVE ME ALL ALONE IN THIS VILLAGE!
BUT YOU'RE PERFECTLY SAFE!

AND WE HAVE TO KNOW WHAT BROUGHT YOU HERE, AND FIND OUT HOW TRAGICOMIX IS!

I COULDN'T CARE LESS ABOUT TRAGICOMIX!
?!

PANACEA IS RIGHT! TRAGICOMIX ALWAYS HAD A MANIA FOR GETTING INTO TROUBLE!*
PLEASE, OBELIX, DON'T COMPLICATE THINGS!
* SEE "ASTERIX THE LEGIONARY"

YOU'RE THE ONE COMPLICATING THINGS, MISTER ASTERIX!!!
WANT TO KNOW WHAT MISTER ASTERIX THINKS YOU ARE?
18A

AND WHAT DOES THAT LITTLE SQUIRT THINK I AM?
HE THINKS YOU'RE A GREAT FAT IDIOT!

I AM NOT FAT!
PAF!

OH, WHAT HAVE I DONE? I ACTUALLY HIT ASTERIX! WHAT A TERRIBLE THING TO DO!

I'M SO SORRY, ASTERIX! I JUST WASN'T THINKING!!

YOU HURT MY FRIEND ASTERIX! I DON'T LIKE YOU ANY MORE, OBELIX!
18B

COME ALONG, ASTERIX, YOU POOR LITTLE THING! WE DON'T WANT ANYTHING MORE TO DO WITH HIM!
WOO-ER!

COME ALONG, DOGMATIX! WE DON'T WANT ANYTHING MORE TO DO WITH THEM!
GRRRR!

YOU KNOW, ASTERIX REALLY GETS ME DOWN! HE ALWAYS HAS TO BE RIGHT!

BUT I OUGHT NOT TO HAVE LOST MY TEMPER!

I'M VERY UNHAPPY, DOGMATIX! I WENT AND HIT MY BEST FRIEND...

...AND PANACEA DOESN'T LIKE ME ANY MORE! BOOHOOHOO!

I HEAR YOU OWN A MAGNIFICENT SWORD, ASTERIX!?
WOO-ER!

SUPPOSE I ASKED YOU FOR THAT SWORD, WOULD YOU GIVE IT TO ME?
WOO-ER!

OH, YOU'RE SUCH A SWEETIE, ASTERIX!
WOO-ER!

COME ON, LET'S GO AND FIND THAT NICE SWORD!
WOO-ER!

ASTERIX!
HAVE YOU BEEN DRINKING?!
WOO-ER!
OH NO!

AREN'T YOU ASHAMED OF YOURSELF? IF YOUR FATHER COULD SEE YOU NOW!!
WOO-ER!
SEE YOU LATER, THEN, ASTERIX!

PSSST! HOW'S IT GOING?
NO LUCK THIS TIME, BUT I'M NOT BEATEN YET!

I'M SURE IT WAS THAT LITTLE MADAM'S FAULT YOU WERE DRINKING!!
GLUG... WOO-ER!

WHATEVER I DO I CAN'T GET HIM BACK TO NORMAL! I'LL GO AND ASK VANILLA TO HELP ME!
20A

I'M WORRIED, VANILLA! ASTERIX HAS COME HOME WITH PANACEA IN A VERY STRANGE STATE!
MY LAD'S IN A STRANGE STATE TOO! HE WON'T FINISH UP HIS NICE SOUP, EVEN GARNISHED WITH ROAST BOAR!

THAT PANACEA IS BAD NEWS FOR OUR BOYS!
YES. I THINK WE'D BETTER CONSULT THE DRUID GETAFIX. HIS WISDOM WILL COME TO OUR AID!

PSST! IT'S ALL RIGHT, THE COAST IS CLEAR!

WHERE ARE YOU GOING THIS TIME PANACEA?!
DON'T WORRY, SOPORIF... I MEAN DAD!

THE MORE I SEE OF MY DAUGHTER, THE LESS LIKE HERSELF SHE SEEMS!
20B

OBELIX'S TROUBLE IS EASY TO DIAGNOSE! HE'S IN LOVE!
GLOP! GLOP!
!

BUT I'LL HAVE TO EXAMINE ASTERIX! MY POTION'S READY, SO I CAN COME WITH YOU NOW!

MIND, I DON'T GUARANTEE THAT THE POTION WILL WORK, BUT AT LEAST ASTERIX IS USED TO TAKING IT!
I'M GOING HOME TO COMFORT MY OBELIXIKINS!

HI! IT'S ME, PANACEA! REMEMBER WHAT YOU PROMISED ME, ASTERIX?
WOO-ER!
21A

RIGHT, SO WHERE'S THAT NICE SWORD?
WOO-ER!

WATCH OUT! HIS MOTHER'S COMING!
GIVE ME THE SWORD, YOU FOOL!
WOO-ER!

WELL?
THAT GREAT BIG BRUTE HIT HIM SO HARD HE'S LOST HIS MEMORY, AND IN HIS CASE IT'S NOT AN ACT!

YOU'D BETTER WATCH OUT IF I FIND YOU HANGING AROUND ASTERIX AGAIN, PANACEA!!!
REMEMBER YOU HAVE A HUSBAND BY THE NAME OF TRAGICOMIX!

OH, GO BACK TO YOUR BORING OLD BOARS AND STOP HAMMING IT UP, BEFORE I SHAKE THE DUST OF THIS PLACE OFF MY COTHURNI*!
* FOOTWEAR OF ROMAN ACTORS ON STAGE

LIFE IN THE BIG CITY CERTAINLY CHANGES PEOPLE A LOT!
21B

SOME GREAT EMOTIONAL SHOCK MUST HAVE LEFT HIM IN THIS STATE!
WOO-ER!

BUT EMOTIONAL OR NOT, HE CERTAINLY NEEDS HELP!
GLUP! WOO-ER! GLUP!

YAHOOOOOOO!
22A

YIPPEEE!
POC!

COME BACK HERE THIS MINUTE, ASTERIX!
?!
YIPPEE
?!?
?!?
?!
FULLIAVTOMATIX
UNHYGIENIX
22B

OH, WONDERFUL STUFF, YOUR POTION! NOW MY SON THINKS HE'S A GIANT FLEA!!!
I HAVE TO CONFESS I DIDN'T FORESEE THESE SPECIAL EFFECTS.

WELL, DO SOMETHING, DON'T JUST STAND THERE TWIDDLING YOUR THUMBS!!!
LISTEN, SARSAPARILLA! I MAY HAVE INVENTED A POTION WHICH GIVES PEOPLE SUPERHUMAN STRENGTH, AND ANOTHER WHICH TURNS THEM INTO GRANITE AND MAKES THEM REVERT TO CHILDHOOD, BUT DO YOU EXPECT ME TO WORK MIRACLES?

YOU SEE, DOGMATIX, WITHOUT ASTERIX I FEEL AS IF THE STUFFING WAS KNOCKED OUT OF ME!

WHOOMPH!
BONG!
22C

ASTERIX!
I'M SO GLAD TO SEE YOU!!!

THIS MUST MEAN YOU'VE FORGIVEN ME! WILL YOU SHAKE ME BY THE HAND?
YAP!

PAF! PAF! PAF! PAF!

WELL, NOBODY COULD SAY THAT WAS NO GREAT SHAKES!

HEY, ASTERIX, WE'RE STILL FRIENDS, RIGHT?
TOC!
23A

ASTERIX! DROPPING IN AT JUST THE RIGHT MOMENT!
PAF!

I HOPE YOU HAVEN'T FORGOTTEN YOUR PROMISE?

OH, I GET THE IDEA! YOU WANT ME TO DANCE WITH YOU IN EXCHANGE!
!?

FLOP! FLOP! FLOP! FLOP! FLOP! FLOP! FLOP! FLOP! FLOP!

OOOOOH! I FEEL SO DIZZY!

!?
SMACK!
23B

HOW DARE YOU, YOU LITTLE

ASTERIX, YOUR BEHAVIOUR IS UNWORTHY OF A GAUL! APOLOGISE AT ONCE! I INSIST!

YIPPEEE!

YIPPEE IS NOT GOOD ENOUGH! APOLOGISE UNLESS YOU WANT TO GET CLOSELY ACQUAINTED WITH THIS FIST AGAIN!!!

YAHOO!
TCHOC!
!?
24A

WELL, I NEVER! WELL, I NEVER!

YOU'RE NOTHING BUT BARBARIANS, THE LOT OF YOU!
YIPPEEE!

OKAY, SO I HIT HIM FIRST, BUT THAT'S NO REASON! AND THIS TIME PANACEA DIDN'T EVEN COMFORT ME! IT'S NOT FAIR!

THE BAND'S STOPPED PLAYING! NOW TO FACE THE MUSIC!
LIKE THE GAULS, LET'S HOPE THE SKY DOESN'T FALL ON OUR HEADS!

CRAASH!
24B

WHAT ON EARTH WAS THAT? WHAT IN THE WORLD WAS THAT?
YAHOO

OOOOOO!
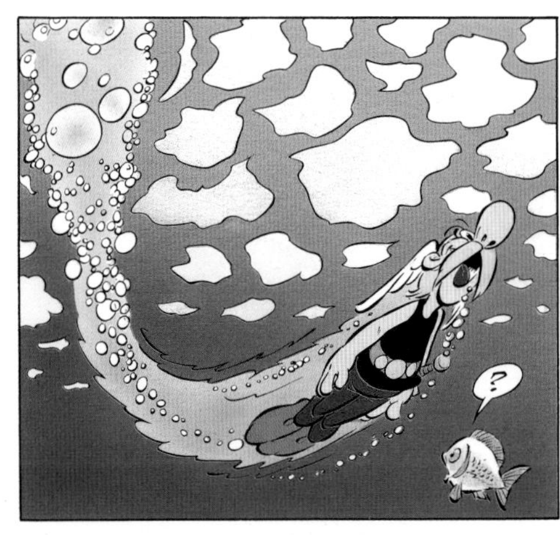
?

YIPPEE!

YOOHOOHOOHOOHOOHOOHOOOO
25A

CLONK!

SEVERAL HOURS LATER...
?!?

...AS THE SEA RISES AND A STORM IS BREWING...
OUCH! MY POOR HEAD! I FEEL AS IF THE SKY FELL ON IT!!!

HEY... WHAT AM I DOING IN THE MIDDLE OF THE SEA, UP A ROCK WITHOUT A PADDLE? THIS IS A NIGHTMARE!
25B

WE'RE A LONG WAY FROM THE COAST WHERE THAT CANTANKEROUS LITTLE GAUL LIVES, BUT WE'D BETTER BE CAREFUL ALL THE SAME!
CETERARUM RERUM PRUDENS!

I SEE A SHIP OVER THERE! I'M SAVED!

AHOY! AHOY THERE!

THE GAU... THE GAUGAU...

CRAASH!
WHAT DO YOU MEAN, THE GAULS? WHAT DO YOU MEAN, THE GAULS? I DON'T SEE ANY GAULS, DO YOU?
SO WHAT DO YOU THINK THAT IS, THEN ???
26A

IT'S A GHOST!
I SPY A SPOOK!

BEAR HARD TO STARBOARD!!!
I'M GOING ASHORE FOR PSYCHOANALYSIS!
?!

SPECTRAL ANALYSIS MIGHT DO THE TRICK, CAP'N!
26 B

SEEMS I'VE GOT NO OPTION! I'M A LONG WAY FROM LAND, BUT I MUST TRY TO SWIM ASHORE!

MUCH LATER, AS THE STORM RAGES EVER MORE VIOLENTLY...
I'M EXHAUSTED! IF TOUTATIS DOESN'T COME TO MY AID...

...I'M DONE FOR...

GLUG!
27A

GASP! GASP!

TOUTATIS HAS SENT ME THIS DOLPHIN!

THANKS, MATE!
CLICKCLICK CLICKCLICK
27B

YOU HAD US REALLY WORRIED, ASTERIX!
I CAN'T MAKE IT OUT. IF THAT HEAVEN-SENT DOLPHIN HADN'T PICKED UP MY SCENT...
OH, MY POOR RIXIKINS!

NEVER MIND THE RECENT PAST FOR NOW, ASTERIX! IN THE IMMEDIATE FUTURE YOU MUST GO TO CONDATUM TO FIND YOUR FATHER!
THAT'S RIGHT... I REMEMBER DISCUSS-ING IT WITH OBELIX!

AND I'VE MADE YOU A GOURD OF MAGIC POTION FOR YOUR JOURNEY!
OH, NO! YOU'RE NOT GOING TO SCOFF ANY MORE OF THAT EVIL BREW ARE YOU, ASTERIX?!!

MADAM, BEFORE YOU SCOFF AT MY EVIL BREW, RECOLLECT THAT THE HAPPY END OF YOUR RIXIKINS' ADVENTURES DEPENDS ON IT, SO AS A MOTHER WILL YOU KINDLY KEEP MUM!!!

GO AND FIND OBELIX! HE NEEDS YOUR SUPPORT JUST NOW, ASTERIX!

THAT GREAT GOOF MUST BE IN THE QUARRY WITH HIS MENHIRS!
TAP
28A

WELL, OBELIX, WE'RE OFF TO CONDATUM, LAND OF OUR FATHERS! COMING?
I DUNNO!

FORGIVE ME IF I HURT YOU, OBELIX! MAYBE I DIDN'T KNOW WHAT I WAS DOING?!
I THINK YOU KNEW PERFECTLY WELL WHAT YOU WERE DOING! AND I THINK YOU RATHER EN-JOYED IT!

COME ON, OBELIX! TRAGICOMIX AND OUR FATHERS MAY NEED US!
VERY WELL, BUT SWEAR THAT YOU WON'T INSULT PANACEA'S DIG-NITY AGAIN!

I DON'T KNOW WHAT YOU'RE ON ABOUT, BUT YES, OF COURSE I SWEAR!
GOOD! WILL YOU SHAKE ME BY THE HAND?

PAF!
PAF!
PAF!
PAF!

WELL, NOBODY COULD SAY THAT WAS NO GREAT SHAKES!
HO, HO, HO! COPYCAT!
28B

IN CONDATUM, WHERE NIGHT HAS FALLEN...
WOW, DID I EVER HAVE A THIRSHT ON ME... HIC, HAEC, HOC!... BACK IN THE PREFECT'S PRISHON!
TAVERN

FACT IS, THEY WEREN'T PLEASHED I DID A DEAL WITH POMPEY'S SHWORD AND ... HIC!... HELMET... BOTTOMSH UP! HEE, HEE, HEE!

IT'S LATE. TIME FOR BED, TREMENSDELIRIUS!
POMPEY ISN'T PLEASHED EITHER... HIC! ... HE'S AFRAID CAESHAR WILL FIND OUT HE'SH IN GAUL ... HIC! ... TO RAISHE AN ARMY AGAINSHT HIM... HIC! TEEHEEHEE...

I SHEEM TO REMEMBER I WAS SHUPPOSHED TO WARN SHOMEONE... HIC!... CAN'T RE-MEMBER WHO... HIC!... 'BOUT CAN'T REMEMBER WHAT! HIC!

SNORRR! ZZZZZ!
29A

A LITTLE LATER, AT THE HEADQUARTERS OF THE LEGATE COMMANDING THE REGION...
WHAT?
LEGATORIA PROVINCIA

QUICK! I WANT A MESSENGER SENT TO CAESAR IN ROME!

AND ONCE AGAIN WE HAVE A PRIVILEGED VIEW OF...
I

...THE MAGNIFICENT ORGANISATION OF THE ROMAN ARMY...

...EVEN IF SOMETIMES...
JUST LET ME GET MY HANDS ON THE SON OF A ... WHO STOLE MY HORSE...
XI
29B

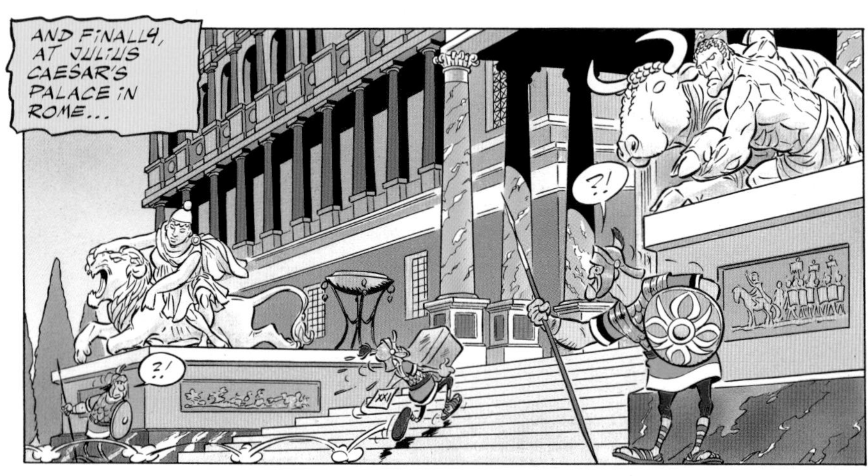
AND FINALLY, AT JULIUS CAESAR'S PALACE IN ROME...
?!
?!
XXI

AN URGENT MESSAGE FOR CAESAR!
ARRRRRRG! WHEEEZE! ARRRRRRG! WHEEZE!
XXI

BY JUPITER! POMPEY!!! NOT HIM AGAIN?

AN URGENT MESSAGE FOR THE LEGATE IN CONDATUM!

AND YET AGAIN WE CAN ADMIRE THE EFFICIENCY OF THE ROMAN POSTAL SERVICE IN ACTION, IN THE OTHER DIRECTION.
THEY SAY THEY'RE GOING TO STOP THE PRICE OF A NEW HORSE FROM MY PAY! TALK ABOUT A RUN OF BAD LUCK!
ROMA
XXI

THE LAST RUNNER FINALLY RELAYS CAESAR'S MESSAGE TO THE LEGATE IN CONDATUM.
ARRRRRRG! WHEEEEZE! ARRRRRRG! WHEEEEZE!
KNOCK KNOCK KNOCK KNOCK

GENTLEMEN, YOU WILL NOW BE AWARE THAT POMPEY IS HERE IN GAUL TO RAISE AN ARMY AGAINST CAESAR, WHO ORDERS US TO INVESTIGATE ALL THE GARRISONS AND FIND THE TRAITORS! SO GET MOVING!

MEANWHILE, STILL IN CONDATUM...
I THINK I'LL CALL ON ASTERIX AND OBELIX'S PARENTS. IT'S A LONG TIME SINCE I LAST SAW THEM!
FOR THIS IS THE REAL PANACEA!
?!
MODERNIT

THE PREFECT'S GUARDS TOOK ASTRONOMIX AND OBELISCOIDIX AWAY! I NEVER SAW THEM AGAIN!

HIRE CHARIOTS
TRAGICOMIX
?!
OH, TRAGICOMIX!! ASTRONOMIX AND OBELISCOIDIX ARE IN DANGER!

WE MUST GO TO THE VILLAGE AT ONCE AND WARN ASTERIX AND OBELIX!
CLAC!

AT THIS VERY MOMENT, IN THE VILLAGE...
I FINALLY MANAGED TO MAKE OFF WITH THE SWORD WHILE ASTERIX AND HIS MOTHER WERE OUT!
THEN LET'S GET OUT OF HERE, QUICK!

WE WANT TO ASK YOU A FAVOUR, ROMAN!
GULP
31A

WE HAVE TO GO TO CONDATUM! WOULD YOU LEND US YOUR CART? IT WOULD GET US THERE FASTER!
ER...WELL... THE FACT IS...

I WAS JUST ASKING FASTANDFURIUS TO TAKE ME BACK TO CONDATUM MYSELF! WE CAN TRAVEL TOGETHER!
I'LL HARNESS UP THE HORSES!
I'M GLAD TO HEAR YOU'VE CHANGED YOUR MIND, PANACEA!

BUT NOT SO LONG AGO SHE WAS SAYING...
LA DONNA È MOBILE, OBELIX!

LATER, ON THE WAY TO CONDATUM...
DID YOU REALLY HAVE TO LUMBER US WITH A MENHIR?
SO? I CAN GIVE MY DAD A PRESENT IF I WANT TO, RIGHT?

YOU DON'T SEEM QUITE YOURSELF, OBELIX, OLD FRIEND!
I'M SAD! I'VE LOST MY LITTLE DOGMATIX!
31B

IN ONE OF THE MANY ROMAN GARRISONS ON OCCUPIED ARMORICAN SOIL...

CENTURION GYMNASTICAPPARATUS, YOUR ORDERS ARE TO INVESTIGATE THE WHOLE SECTOR IN ORDER TO IDENTIFY AND EXPOSE THE LEGIONS IN POMPEY'S PAY!
IT WON'T BE EASY IF THEY DON'T HAVE ANY DISTINGUISHING MARKS, GENERAL!

NEVER MIND THAT! GET MOVING!!!
?!

DECURION COUGHLINCTUS! YOU AND YOUR MEN ARE TO COMB THE WHOLE SECTOR AND PICK UP POMPEIANS, WHO ARE LEGION HERE!
JUST AS YOU SAY, CENTURION, BUT 'SCUSE ME ASKING, HOW DO I RECOGNISE A POMPARIAN WHEN I SEE ONE?

NEVER MIND THAT! GET MOVING!!!
POP!

GOT IT, YOU BUNCH OF SKIVERS? WE COMB THE SECTOR, WE PICK UP ALL THE POMPARIANS WE FIND, AND WE REPORT BACK. ANY QUESTIONS?

NEVER MIND THAT! GET MOVING!!!
?!
?!
?!
?!
?!
?!
?!
?!
?!
?!

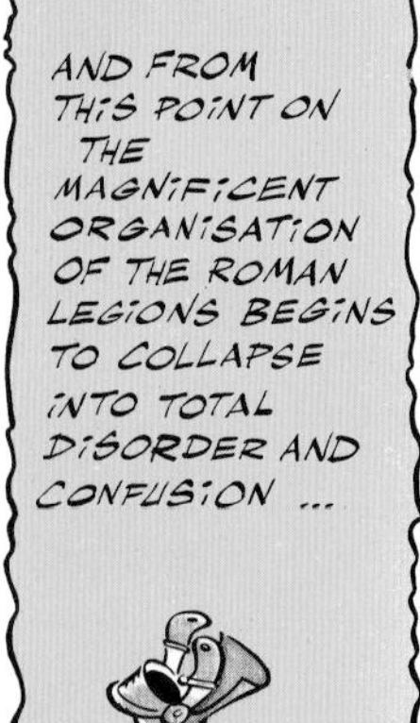
AND FROM THIS POINT ON THE MAGNIFICENT ORGANISATION OF THE ROMAN LEGIONS BEGINS TO COLLAPSE INTO TOTAL DISORDER AND CONFUSION ...

HALT! WHO GOES THERE? ARE YOU THE POMPARIAN LEGIONARIES WE'RE AFTER? IF SO, IT'S A FAIR COP!
YOU'LL BE COPPING IT YOURSELF IF YOU DON'T WATCH OUT!

MIND YOUR MANNERS, YOU GREAT FAT WINESKIN!
GREAT FAT WINESKIN YOURSELF!

YOU'LL SOON BE SLEEPING IT OFF IN THE CAN!
WHILE YOU KICK YOUR HEELS AT YOUR OWN CONVENIENCE!*
33A
* PROPHETIC REFERENCE TO A SMALL ROOM NOT YET INVENTED

GET THIS BUNCH OF YOBBOS UNDER ARREST!
?!
COME ON, LAY INTO THEM!

ROMANS FIGHTING EACH OTHER???
HAVE THESE ROMANS GONE CRAZY?!
PIF!
BANG!
THUD
THUD! BANG!
33B

IT'S NOT FAIR, ROMANS FIGHTING AMONGST THEMSELVES!
GLUG! GLUG! GLUG!

LETS MAKE THEM SEE REASON!

AREN'T YOU ASHAMED OF YOURSELVES, THUMPING EACH OTHER?
WITHOUT WAITING FOR US?

WE'RE NOT INTERESTED IN YOU, GAULS!
YEAH! WE'VE GOT OTHER FISH TO FRY!
TAP! TAP!

WOULD YOU LIKE THEM BATTERED?
TAKE THAT ... YOU'VE HAD YOUR CHIPS!
CRACK!
CLONK!
34A

WHOOOOSH!

CRAAAAAASH!

RIGHT, THE ROAD'S CLEAR NOW!
ASTERIX! THE CART HAS DISAPPEARED !??

THEY... THEY'VE LEFT US BEHIND!
34B

FUNNY THING FOR FASTANDFURIUS TO DO!
YOU BET! AND PANACEA IS HIS PRISONER! WE MUST CATCH UP WITH HIM!

YOU KNOW, PANACEA'S OWN BEHAVIOUR SINCE SHE CAME HOME BAFFLES ME!
ME TOO! SHE'S BEEN MUCH COOLER TO ME THAN USUAL!

YOU NEVER CEASE TO SURPRISE ME, OBELIX! BUT WE'LL HAVE TROUBLE CATCHING UP WITH THEM, IN SPITE OF THE WEIGHT OF YOUR MENHIR!

WE'D GO FASTER WITHOUT THAT MENHIR! YOU OUGHT TO CHUCK IT OUT, FASTANDFURIUS!

LOOK, I'M CORRUPT, A DECEIVER, A LIAR AND A CONSPIRATOR, SO WHO AM I TO CAST THE FIRST STONE?

JUPITER'S THUNDERBOLTS!
35A

MAKE WAY, GAUL! I'M IN A HURRY!
AND SO AM I, ROMAN!

WHAT THE...? PANACEA?

??
YES, WHAT IS IT, TRAGICOMIX?

?
35B

IT'S THE REAL PANACEA! WE'RE FINISHED!
NOT YET! LEAVE THIS TO ME!

WHO ARE YOU? AND WHY THIS MASQUERADE?

I ... I'M ONLY A HUMBLE MENHIR DELIVERY-MAN AND I ... I'M HAPPY TO MAKE WAY FOR YOU!

I ONLY KNOW ONE MENHIR DELIVERY-MAN, AND HE'S NOT A RAT-BAG LIKE YOU!

OH, PLEASE DON'T HURT ME! I'M A TERRIBLE COWARD!
WHAT IS THAT WOMAN DOING DISGUISED AS PANACEA? WHO IS SHE?

HULLO, HANDSOME! DON'T YOU RECOGNISE YOUR OWN LITTLE PANACEA?
36A

I'LL SHOW YOU HIS OWN LITTLE PANACEA!!!

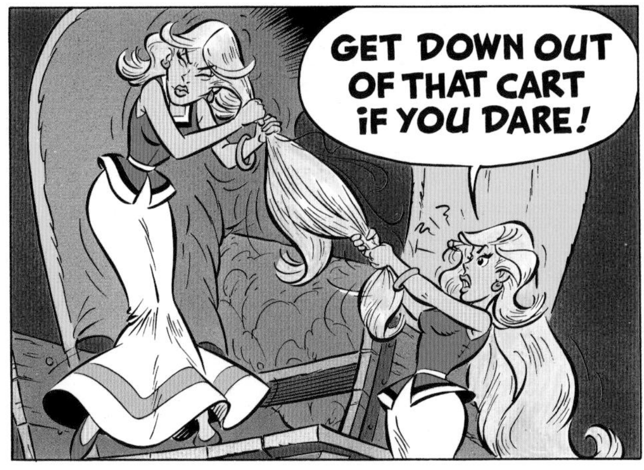
GET DOWN OUT OF THAT CART IF YOU DARE!

?!

IT ... IT'S A WIG!!!

OH, VERY WELL! I AM THE GREAT ROMAN TRAGIC ACTRESS AND OPERATIC DIVA LATRAVIATA! NO NEED TO MAKE A GREAT SONG AND DANCE ABOUT IT!
?!?
?!?
36B

?!
COOEEE!
WE'RE SURPRISED TO SEE YOU, TRAGICOMIX, BUT PLEASED TOO!
SAME HERE, ASTERIX! MAYBE YOU CAN HELP ME GET A FEW THINGS CLEARED UP!

ANY IDEA WHY THIS ACTRESS WAS PRETENDING TO BE PANACEA?
?!?

NOW I UNDERSTAND THE PECULIAR WAY SHE WAS ACTING!
BUT THEN... SHE WASN'T THE REAL PANACEA AFTER ALL!
HERE'S THE REAL PANACEA, OBELIX DEAR!

OH, ASTERIX, FORGIVE ME! I THOUGHT YOU...
37A

THE ROMAN! HE'S MAKING A BREAK FOR IT!

NO, OBELIX! DON'T!
I'M ABOUT TO LOSE MY TEMPER!

BONG!

ALL RIGHT, ROMAN?
WOO-ER!

THE PREFECT OF CONDATUM SENT ME TO RECOVER POMPEY'S SWORD AND HELMET! BUT MY PART IS OVER NOW! HERE ARE THE SWORD AND HELMET BACK... THOUGH I'M AFRAID THAT HEAVY MENHIR IN THE CART...
THOSE WEAPONS MUST HAVE SOMETHING TO DO WITH YOUR FATHERS' IMPRISONMENT BY THE PREFECT, ASTERIX!!!
!
37B

OH, LET THE ROMANS SETTLE THEIR OWN DIFFERENCES! IT'S NONE OF OUR BUSINESS, OBELIX!

ALL THE SAME... WHAT A WASTE!

PAF! BONG! THUD! PIF!

CONDATE

AND FINALLY, IN CONDATUM...
?!

NO PARKING OUTSIDE THE PREFECTURE!
OBELIX, WOULD YOU TELL THE ROMAN POLITELY THAT WE WON'T BE HERE FOR LONG?
YES, OF COURSE!

...IF YOU DON'T MIND!
PAF!

GUARDS! RAISE THE ALARM!
AT LAST! SOMEONE WHO KNOWS THE RULES!
GLUG! GLUG! GLUG!

YOU'VE NO IDEA HOW POLITE I FEEL JUST NOW!
KERPLONK!
CRAAASH!

BING! PAF! PIF! BONG!
IT'S ABOUT TIME TO GET OUT OF HERE AND FIND POMPEY!

WOULD YOU BE KIND ENOUGH TO TELL ME WHERE THE PREFECT IS HOLDING THE TWO GAULISH MERCHANTS PRISONER?
WITH... WITH FPLEATHURE... IN THE DUNGEONTH, THELL X!

YOU'RE RIGHT, ASTERIX! A LITTLE TOUGH LOVE NEVER HURT ANYONE!

GAULS RUNNING ABOUT FREE IN MY PRISON ?!? QUIS, QUID, UBI, QUIBUS AUXILIIS, CUR, QUOMODO, QUANDO ???

CRASH!
ONLY PASSING THROUGH!

ASTERIX, OBELIX! AT LAST!!!
DAD!

I FELT I WAS GROWING OLD DOWN HERE, SON!
MY BABY BOY! IT'S GOOD TO SEE YOU!!

AND HOW'S YOUR MOTHER?
SHE'S JUST FINE, EXCEPT HER ONE IDEA IS TO MARRY ME OFF!
ANY NEWS APART FROM THAT?
40A

!
WELL, BOGUS GENIUS? A RAT LEAVING THE SINKING SHIP?

WELL, PREFECT? LEAVING US WITHOUT SAYING GOODBYE?!
WE TOLD YOU TO WAIT FOR OUR SONS TO TURN UP!
!

STOP THAT TRAITOR!
THOSE ARE THE TRAITORS! THEY'VE GOT POMPEY'S WEAPONS!
I THINK WE'LL HAVE TO BE VERY, VERY POLITE TO THEM AGAIN, OBELIX!

YOU KNOW WHAT? I SHALL NEVER REGRET VISITING CONDATUM!
40B

WELL, GAULS, I CERTAINLY SEEM TO BUMP INTO YOU WHENEVER THINGS ARE GOING BADLY!

HI, JULES! I KNOW ABOUT YOUR PROBLEMS, BUT THEY'RE NOTHING TO DO WITH US. WE GAULS AREN'T INTERESTED IN POLITICAL INFIGHTING AMONG ROMANS!

41B

I KNOW, BUT ALL THE SAME, CAN YOU TELL ME IF YOU HAPPEN TO HAVE SEEN POMPEY AND THAT TRAITOR BOGUS GENIUS?
YES, OF COURSE!

I MET BOGUS GENIUS A MOMENT AGO, AND HE'S JUST MET RATHER A LOT OF LEGIONARIES HIMSELF. AS FOR POMPEY...

WOULD THIS BE THE MAN YOU'RE AFTER, CAESAR?

HE RAN INTO ME JUST NOW. HE SEEMED TO BE IN A HURRY TO LEAVE CONDATUM!

SINCE IT'S A CHANGE OF AIR THEY'RE AFTER, I'LL HAVE THEM SHIPPED OFF TO THE DESERTS OF AFRICA. THAT'LL COOL THEM DOWN A BIT!
42A

AND LET IT NEVER BE SAID THAT CAESAR WAS UNGRATEFUL! GAULS, YOU DESERVE THE TROPHY I AM GOING TO GIVE YOU!

IT'S A GOLDEN ME!
WHAT'S A GOLDEN MEAN?
HE SAID A GOLDEN ME... PROBABLY A GOLDEN STATUE OF HIMSELF!

THANKS, JULES, BUT THE PERSON WHO REALLY DESERVES A TROPHY...
?!?

...IS THE GREAT ACTRESS LATRAVIATA, WHO HAS GIVEN US A DEMONSTRATION OF HER HISTRIONIC GENIUS!

GIVE A WOMAN A TROPHY FOR ACTING? THAT'S RIDICULOUS!
42B

LATER...
WE'LL HAVE OUR WORK CUT OUT, GETTING THIS PLACE STRAIGHT AGAIN!
OH, MANY HANDS MAKE LIGHT WORK!
I MUST ASK YOU TO FORGIVE ME FOR MY PART IN ALL THIS...

WE BEAR NO GRUDGES...
AND WE'RE GOING TO GIVE YOU...
?!

...SOMETHING...
...WHICH WILL SUIT YOU DOWN TO THE GROUND!

A ROMAN LADY LEFT THIS ROBE WITH US. SHE LOST EVERYTHING BUT HER SANDALS AT DICE!
43A

AND A LITTLE LATER STILL...
CLAP! CLAP!
CLAP! CLAP!
CLAP! CLAP! CLAP! CLAP! CLAP! CLAP! CLAP!

I SHALL NEVER FORGET THE GENEROSITY OF THOSE SO UNJUSTLY DESCRIBED AS BARBARIANS!

AND NOW I MUST LEAVE YOU. I'M GETTING FASTANDFURIUS TO TAKE ME BACK TO ROME.
WOO-ER!
HE LOOKS STONED OUT OF HIS MIND! ONE OF YOUR MENHIRS, WAS IT?
WELL, ONLY A LITTLE ONE!

GOODBYE, ASTERIX! THANKS TO YOU, THIS GOLDEN TROPHY WILL OPEN THE DOORS OF EVERY THEATRE IN ROME TO ME!
OH, IT WAS NOTHING!

SMACK!
43B

"QUID NOVI" UNDER THE STARRY SKY OF GAUL? NOTHING REALLY, JUST THE TRADITIONAL REJOICINGS IN THE VILLAGE TO MARK THE RETURN OF OUR HEROES, WITH A LAVISH BANQUET ... PLENTY OF ROAST WILD BOARS, MUCH TO THE SATISFACTION OF A GAUL WHO ISN'T FAT, JUST WELL COVERED. THE ONLY OTHER THING HE WANTS IS TO BE REUNITED WITH HIS FOUR-FOOTED FRIEND... AND THAT MOMENT IS FAST APPROACHING...

LADIES AND GENTLEMEN, GAULS AND FRIENDS, I RAISE MY DRINKING HORN TO...

SCRUNCH! SCRUNCH!

OBELISCOIDIX! YOU KNOW YOU OUGHT TO WATCH YOUR DIET!

DO REMEMBER THAT BARLEY BEER DOESN'T AGREE WITH YOU, ASTRONOMIX!

I'M SO GLAD TO HAVE OUR DADS HERE TOO, OBELIX!

SCRUNCH! SCRUNCH!

I SHAN'T FEEL REALLY HAPPY UNTIL MY LITTLE DOGMATIX TURNS UP, ASTERIX!

SPECIAL OFFER

UDERZO 2000

44B

R. GOSCINNY Asterix A. UDERZO

Asterix and the class act

Written by René GOSCINNY and Albert UDERZO

Illustrated by Albert UDERZO

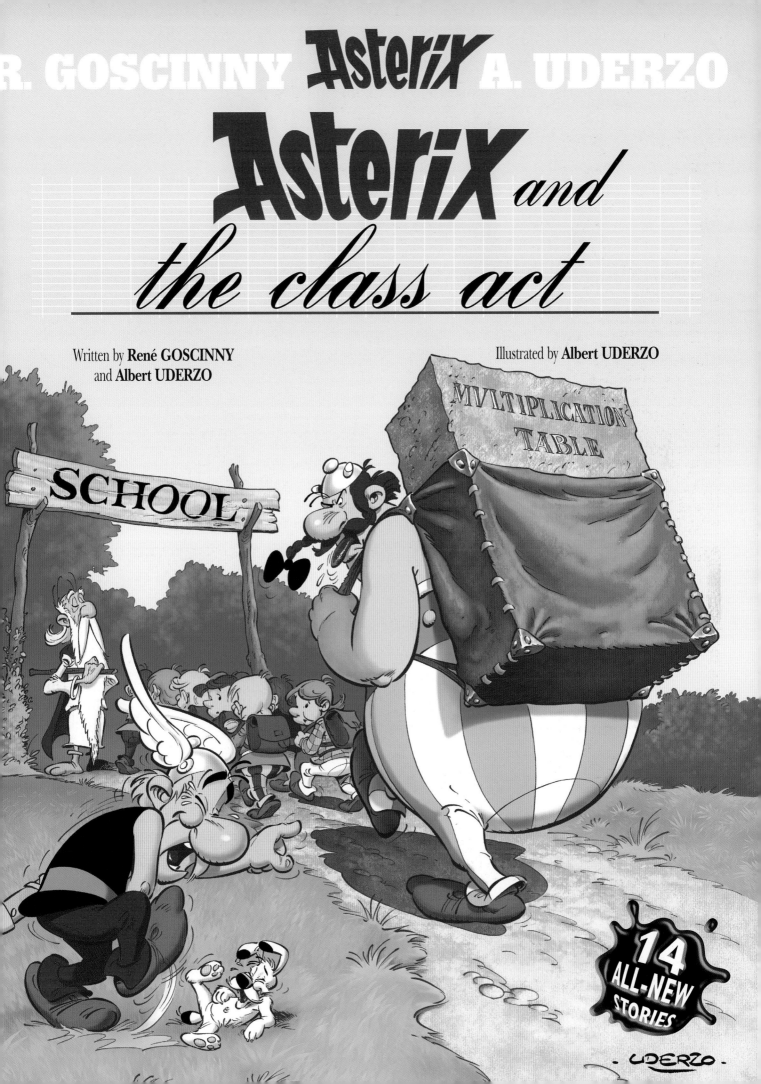

GOSCINNY AND UDERZO

PRESENT

Fourteen all-new Asterix stories

Asterix and the class act

Written by RENÉ GOSCINNY *and* ALBERT UDERZO

Illustrated by ALBERT UDERZO

Translated by ANTHEA BELL *and* DEREK HOCKRIDGE

The French publisher's note

During the 1960s, when René Goscinny and Albert Uderzo had time to spare from writing and drawing the longer Asterix adventures ... which was not very often ... they produced some little masterpieces in the form of complete short stories. The French magazine "Pilote", enjoyed by a whole generation of children, in which the Asterix stories first appeared, published most but not all of them. Others appeared in such places as American newspapers, a women's magazine, and as part of a bid for the Olympic Games to be held in Paris. It seemed a good idea to collect all these short stories in a special Asterix album — in fact here at Les Éditions Albert René, we were receiving such terrible threats that we absolutely had to do it. If we didn't publish them, said readers, they would make us eat roast boar for breakfast! So we gave in to the outrageous demands of certain blackmailers whose identity we shall have to reveal one of these days.

But for the moment, having brought these lost treasures to light, we hope you will enjoy reading them. Some of the stories in this book are both written and illustrated by Albert on his own, because they were created after the death in 1977 of his friend and colleague, the other half of the most famous strip cartoon team in the world: René Goscinny and Albert Uderzo.

None of these stories had been published in English before, although several were included in our 1993 collection (see page 47 for the full story).

Seeing his publishers absorbed in the difficult but fascinating task of collecting the stories and improving the original picture quality for "Asterix and the Class Act", Albert set to work again. And in the spring of 2003 he produced the cover design and the words and drawings for a brand-new five-page story, about a cockerel with amazing powers. Will the rooster who wakes the Gauls every morning rouse the children of today to get up and go to school for their own class act?

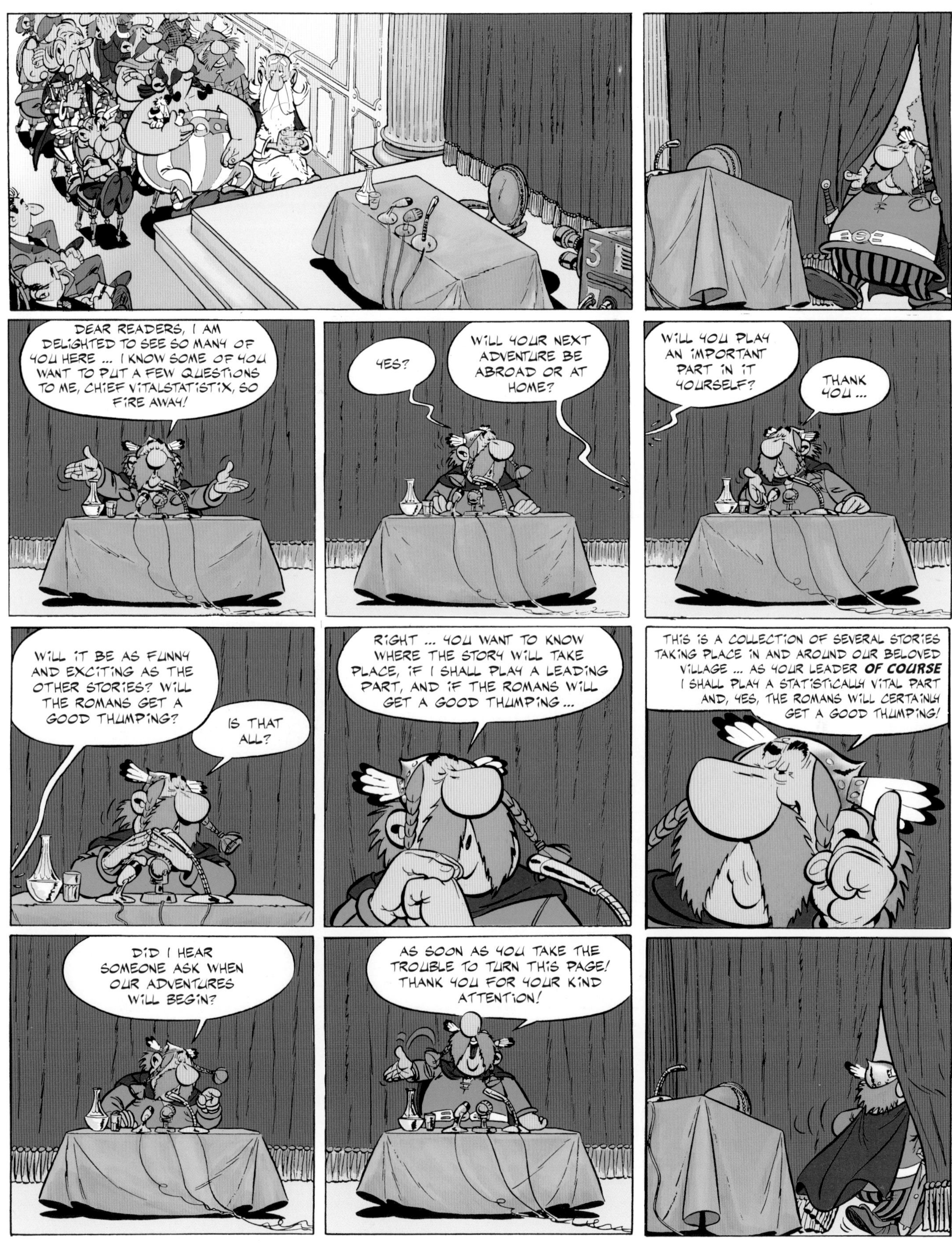
DEAR READERS, I AM DELIGHTED TO SEE SO MANY OF YOU HERE ... I KNOW SOME OF YOU WANT TO PUT A FEW QUESTIONS TO ME, CHIEF VITALSTATISTIX, SO FIRE AWAY!
YES?
WILL YOUR NEXT ADVENTURE BE ABROAD OR AT HOME?
WILL YOU PLAY AN IMPORTANT PART IN IT YOURSELF?
THANK YOU ...
WILL IT BE AS FUNNY AND EXCITING AS THE OTHER STORIES? WILL THE ROMANS GET A GOOD THUMPING?
IS THAT ALL?
RIGHT ... YOU WANT TO KNOW WHERE THE STORY WILL TAKE PLACE, IF I SHALL PLAY A LEADING PART, AND IF THE ROMANS WILL GET A GOOD THUMPING ...
THIS IS A COLLECTION OF SEVERAL STORIES TAKING PLACE IN AND AROUND OUR BELOVED VILLAGE ... AS YOUR LEADER **OF COURSE** I SHALL PLAY A STATISTICALLY VITAL PART AND, YES, THE ROMANS WILL CERTAINLY GET A GOOD THUMPING!
DID I HEAR SOMEONE ASK WHEN OUR ADVENTURES WILL BEGIN?
AS SOON AS YOU TAKE THE TROUBLE TO TURN THIS PAGE! THANK YOU FOR YOUR KIND ATTENTION!

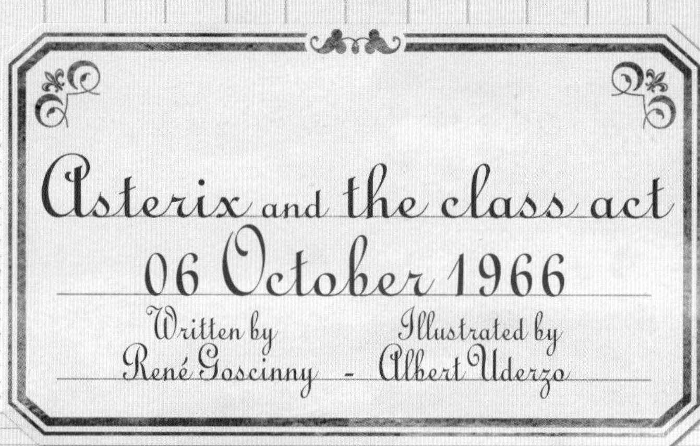

Asterix and the class act
06 October 1966

Written by René Goscinny - Illustrated by Albert Uderzo

The magazine "Pilote" published 52 issues a year, so the editorial team had to rack its brains to think up new stories every week.

When the beginning of the new school year came round, it seemed an ideal subject. René and Albert thought about the logistical problems facing the Gauls in getting their children to school. Here we see them, rather in advance of their time, using the equivalent of the school bus in the year 50 BC. René sat down at his typewriter and soon sent Albert the text. "One of René's talents," Albert Uderzo still remembers, "was a gift for adapting his stories for different artists. Morris hated wordplay, so René didn't use it in the "Lucky Luke" cowboy stories that Morris illustrated. Tabary, who illustrated René's stories about the wicked Arabian Nights vizier "Iznogoud", loved puns, so those books are full of them." There was total sympathy and understanding between René and Albert, who were great friends and equal partners. They never felt the slightest anxiety about the quality of each other's work. The cover of the magazine "Pilote" was created by Albert.

"Pilote", n°363

Asterix and the CLASS ACT
TEXT: GOSCINNY
DRAWINGS: UDERZO
PUT THAT MENHIR DOWN, OBELIX! TODAY'S THE DAY!
WHAT, ALREADY? OH NO!

OH YES, OBELIX! YOU KNOW YOU PUT YOUR MENHIR DOWN ON THIS DAY EVERY YEAR!
THE FACT IS, I FEEL A LITTLE WEAK, ASTERIX, AND...

AND YOU KNOW GETAFIX WANTS US TO PICK UP KIDS, NOT MENHIRS, SO DON'T GROUSE!
GRGNGRGNGRGN GROGNGROGN! I'M NOT GROUSING! I JUST FEEL A LITTLE WEAK!
BONG!

AHA! THERE'S SOMEONE IN THOSE BUSHES!
1A

AAAH! NOOO! MALE CHAUVINIST BOAR!
WHOOSH!

BRUTAL MISOGYNIST!
?

SUCH LANGUAGE! WHERE DO THEY PICK IT UP?

EVERYTHING OKAY, OBELIX?
YOU BET! WE'RE A REAL CLASS ACT!

ONE MORE TRIP AND THAT'LL BE ALL THE TINY TOTS.
HEY! COME HERE, WILL YOU?

COME DOWN! COME DOWN THIS MINUTE, BY BELENOS!
WON'T, BY TOUTATIS, SO THERE!
1B

YOOWWL YOWL!
BUT I HAD TO PICK THE PRETTY TREE, DOGMATIX!
IT'S SOOO UNFAIR! WE'RE THE YOOF CULTURE! LET US DO OUR THING!
THERE WE ARE ... ALL TOTTED UP.

CHILDREN, I'M ASHAMED OF YOU. EVERY NEW SCHOOL YEAR YOU HAVE TO BE ROUNDED UP LIKE WILD BOAR PIGLETS! YOU KNOW YOU MUST GO TO SCHOOL IF YOU'RE TO BE GOOD GAULS!

SO WHY DON'T ASTERIX AND OBELIX GO TO SCHOOL, O DRUID?
THEY DID AT YOUR AGE, AND THEY WORKED HARD. RIGHT, THIS IS CLASSROOM CHALLENGE!
AB
CD

OBELIX, FOR A STARTER: DATE OF THE BATTLE OF GERGOVIA?
UM... ER...
2A

THE BATTLE WE WON?
THE BATTLE WE WON!

MDXV!
WOULD IT BE MDXV?
NO, IT WOULD NOT BE MDXV!

THE BATTLE OF GERGOVIA ...
COME ON, COME ON! I WANT AN ANSWER.

I
+I
=II
2B

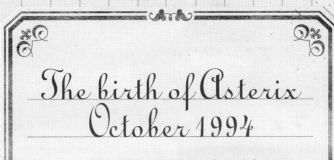

The birth of Asterix
October 1994

Written and illustrated by Albert Uderzo

To celebrate 35 years of Asterix stories, we decided to publish an Asterix Special for the little Gaul's birthday, a one-off magazine in the spirit of "Pilote" in the 1960s. We got together famous names and European authors who wanted to pay tribute to Asterix and his friends. As part of our project, of course, we hoped for a new Asterix story.

It was in a plane bound for Copenhagen in the spring of 1994 that Albert Uderzo told us, with relish, about his idea for an original story to celebrate the birthday. He was already looking forward to revealing the secret of the birth of Asterix and Obelix, and at the same time he told us the names of the older generation: Asterix's parents Astronomix and Sarsaparilla, and Obelix's father and mother Obeliscoidix and Vanilla.

"Le Journal exceptionnel d'Astérix"

IN THE year 35 B.C.*

* BEFORE CAESAR

*ANCIENT GAUL KNOWN FOR HIS LOVE OF LUXURY

FOLLOW YOUR PARENTS' EXAMPLE! SEE HOW THEY RESPECT THE PEACE OF OUR LAW-ABIDING VILLAGE!

A LITTLE LATER...
I THOUGHT I TOLD YOU NOT TO FIGHT YOUR LITTLE FRIENDS!!
A CHIEF'S SON SHOULD SET AN EXAMPLE, BY TOUTATIS!
WELL, THE FACT IS...
ANCIENT TIMES

THE FACT IS WHAT, EH? WHAT?
WELL ... IT WAS FULLIAUTOMATIX'S FAULT. HE'S SEMI-AUTOMATIX'S SON ... HE SAYS HIS DAD SAYS YOU OUGHT TO BE MASTER IN YOUR OWN HOUSE BEFORE BOSSING THE VILLAGE ABOUT!

AND JUST WHERE DO YOU THINK YOU'RE GOING?
FOR A LITTLE WALK ... WON'T BE LONG!

SO I HEAR YOU SAY I OUGHT TO BE MASTER IN MY OWN HOUSE, IS THAT RIGHT?
COULD BE. SO WHAT?
CLANG!
CLANG!

SO THIS!
BONG!

UNHEALTHIX
WELL DONE, CHIEF! YOU SCORED A HIT!

SCHTONG!

SPLATCH!
MISSED!
Fish UNHEALTHIX Shellfish

AND HERE WE SEE THE VERY FIRST IN A LONG SERIES OF FISH FIGHTS IN THE GAULISH VILLAGE.
UNHEALT
YOU SHOULD BE ASHAMED OF YOURSELVES, FIGHTING IN FRONT OF YOUR CHILDREN!

MEANWHILE ...
OFF YOU GO, ASTRONOMIX! THIS IS NO PLACE FOR YOU! LEAVE IT ALL TO US!

DO BE SENSIBLE, OBELISCOIDIX! YOU WON'T BE ANY USE IN THERE!
RRY
COIDIX

IT'S GALLING FOR A GAUL TO BE SO HELPLESS AT A TIME LIKE THIS, DON'T YOU THINK, OBELISCOIDIX?
YUP ... AND WHEN I FEEL GALLED I GET HUNGRY!

SPLATCH!

FOLLOW ME! THIS WILL CALM US DOWN!

STOP THAT! THIS IS NO DAY FOR VULGAR BRAWLS!

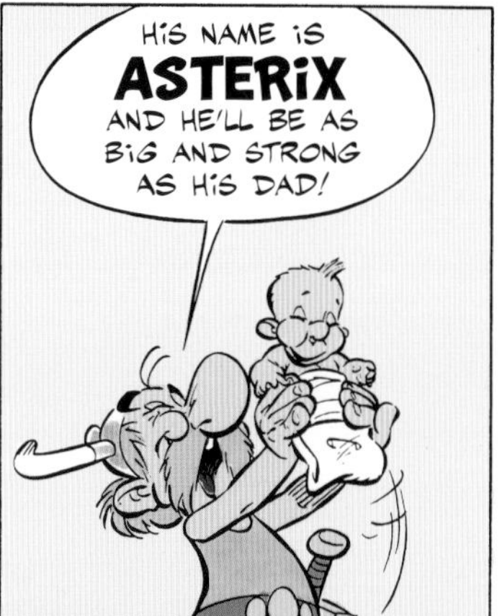

A FEW DAYS AFTER THE BIRTH OF THE TWO BABIES, THE WHOLE VILLAGE MEETS TO CELEBRATE THE HAPPY EVENT. THERE IS A BANQUET, WITH PLENTY OF ROAST WILD BOAR.

WHEN I GROW UP I SHALL SING ODES IN THEIR PRAISE.

OH YETH? WE'LL THEE ABOUT THAT!

ONE OF THEM'S A LOT FATTER THAN THE OTHER.

HE'S NOT FAT, JUST WELL COVERED, THAT'S ALL!

FUNNY, HE SEEMS TO LIKE THE SMELL OF ROAST BOAR ALREADY!

AND 35 YEARS LATER THE ADVENTURES OF ASTERIX AND HIS FAITHFUL COMPANION OBELIX BEGIN. LATER STILL THEY WILL BE TOLD BY TWO OTHER FIRM FRIENDS, HOPING ONLY TO PROVIDE A LITTLE FUN FOR READERS BOTH LARGE AND SMALL.

- UDERZO - 94

4B

In 50 BC
May 1977
Written by
René Goscinny
-
Illustrated by
Albert Uderzo

Georges Dargaud, the publisher of "Pilote" and the Asterix books, wanted to see his leading series reach the American market. The head of an American syndicate visited Paris to meet the creators of the phenomenally successful character Asterix, and they soon came to an agreement. An Asterix album would be published in daily instalments in a number of American papers. René and Albert were delighted but cautious, and thought it might be a good idea to present the world of Asterix to the Americans in an original, condensed form before embarking on the publication of a whole story. The result was these three pages, which for a long time were unknown even in France. Enjoy!

It was the famous "National Geographic" magazine that published them in May 1977, when it was running a major piece about the Gauls. However, the authors' efforts went unrewarded. Publication in American strip cartoon format meant reducing the size of the pictures, which made it difficult to read the speech bubbles. As the authors did not want to have their original work modified beyond the adaptations usual in translation, the experiment ended after the first album — since René and Albert declined an offer for them to go and live in the USA so as to suit their work to the "American format".

"National Geographic"

IN 50 BC
THE ROMAN ARMY
HAD OCCUPIED THE
ENTIRE KNOWN WORLD ...
SPQR

THEIR GENERAL JULIUS CAESAR, NOW AT THE HEIGHT OF HIS POWER, WAS STILL DREAMING OF NEW CONQUESTS ...
ARE YOU QUITE SURE THERE'S NOTHING OVER THERE?
ATLANTIC OCEAN

IN ROME, JULIUS CAESAR WENT FROM TRIUMPH TO TRIUMPH ...

... WITH CAPTIVES FROM DEFEATED NATIONS FOLLOWING HIS CHARIOT IN CHAINS ...
DO YOU THINK THEY'LL GIVE US THE AFTERNOON OFF TO GO SHOPPING?
WILL WE GET TO VISIT THE CIRCUS?
NICE TOWN, I SAY, WHAT, BUT A BIT TOO LATIN FOR MY TASTE!
To fisit it iss not bad, but to liff in I vould it not like.
NO. DID YOU SEE THE PRICES?

AMONG THOSE DEFEATED NATIONS WAS GAUL.

TODAY THE FRENCH LIVE IN GAUL, AND IT IS CALLED FRANCE.
HOW ARE YOU, SIR?
MUSTN'T GRUMBLE WHILE IT KEEPS FINE.
CAFÉ

THE ANCESTORS OF THE FRENCH WERE KNOWN AS GAULS.
HOW ARE YOU, SIR?
MUSTN'T GRUMBLE WHILE THE SKY DOESN'T FALL ON OUR HEADS ...
?

THERE WERE TWO KINDS OF GAULS. SOME HAD ACCEPTED THE RULE OF THE ROMAN INVADER ...
CÆSAR

... AND IMITATED THEIR CONQUERORS' LANGUAGE AND BEHAVIOUR ...
QUO VADIS, DOMINE?
ALEA JACTA EST ...

... AND THE LOVERS OF LIBERTY WHO STILL HELD OUT AGAINST THE INVADERS.
CÆSAR

ONE SUCH GROUP OF GAULS WAS HOLDING OUT IN A TINY VILLAGE ON THE WEST COAST OF THE COUNTRY.

THE ROMANS KEPT A CLOSE WATCH ON THESE CHEERFUL GAULS, WHO LIKED A GOOD LAUGH ...
BY JUPITER, THE GAULS SEEM TO GO IN FOR KNOCKABOUT FARCE!

OF ALL THE VILLAGE WARRIORS, ASTERIX WAS THE MOST INTELLIGENT ...

... AND THE BEST AT UNMASKING ROMAN SPIES.

BY JUPITER, HOW DID HE SEE THROUGH MY CUNNING DISGUISE?
I TOLD YOU OAK TREES DON'T SMELL OF GARLIC, GEORGE!

OBELIX, A MENHIR DELIVERY MAN BY TRADE, IS ASTERIX'S BEST FRIEND.

HISTORIANS HAVE NOT YET FOUND OUT WHAT MENHIRS WERE ACTUALLY FOR.

AND AS FOR THE USE OBELIX OFTEN MAKES OF THEM, THE ROMANS AS WELL AS HISTORIANS ARE AT CROSS PURPOSES.
CROSS, BY JUPITER? I'M FURIOUS! THIS IS NOT WHAT I'D CALL LIGHT BANTER!

LOOK, ASTERIX! I'VE TAUGHT DOGMATIX A NEW TRICK!

THIS MAY SEEM STRANGE, BUT REMEMBER THAT DOG BISCUITS HAD NOT YET BEEN INVENTED IN 50 BC.
SMACK!

LIKE THE OTHER VILLAGERS, DOGMATIX GETS HIS AMAZING STRENGTH FROM THE MAGIC POTION BREWED BY THE DRUID GETAFIX.

THIS MAGIC POTION HAS A SPECTACULAR EFFECT ON THE GAULS ...
YOU KNOW DOGMATIX HATES PEOPLE TO PULL UP TREES!
BUT I ONLY GAVE IT A TINY TAP!

... AND THE ROMANS TOO.
BY JUPITER, THAT GAULISH BREW PACKS A PUNCH!

THE BARD CACOFONIX IS ANOTHER PROMINENT VILLAGER ...
OH TO BE IN ARMORICA NOW THAT APRIL'S ...

... HERE!

... AND SO IS FULLIAUTOMATIX THE BLACKSMITH, WHO IS ALSO PROBABLY THE ANCESTOR OF ALL MUSIC CRITICS.

THE VILLAGE CHIEF IS THE MAJESTIC VITALSTATISTIX ...

THERE'S NO DISCIPLINE IN THIS VILLAGE ANY MORE! NO RESPECT! YOU ARE ALL TO BOW TO ME AND MY AUTHORITY!

BUT CHIEF, YOU SAID YOURSELF ...
I WANTED THE OTHERS TO BOW, YOU FOOLS, NOT YOU!

AS THERE IS NOTHING THE ROMANS CAN DO ABOUT THE SUPERHUMAN STRENGTH OF THE GAULISH VILLAGERS ...
BY JUPITER, TO THINK THERE'S XVIII YEARS TO GO BEFORE I'M DEMOBBED!

THE GAULS (OR MOST OF THEM) REMAIN FREE AND HAPPY.
UDERZO & GOSCINNY

Chanticleerix
August 2003

Written and illustrated by Albert Uderzo

Never before published, this five-page story was finished in May 2003 and is about the village cockerel. It adds to Albert Uderzo's carnival of animals. He has always been particularly fond of chickens. Every Asterix album contains hens and cockerels leading their private and obviously harmonious family lives in the corners of the pictures. The idea for this story came from a projected film spin-off. With René Goscinny, Albert Uderzo once planned a pilot for an animated cartoon film starring Dogmatix – a rarity which has remained unknown. But when he looked at it again 30 years later, Albert thought he would like to write a new story about the birds who share the village with the indomitable Gauls. You might think that the magical forest of Broceliande, not far from the Gaulish village, had given them new powers – but don't tell Obelix!

Gaulish Cockerel

CHANTICLEERIX THE Gaulish Cockerel

UDERZO

IT IS OFTEN THOUGHT THAT ANIMALS HAVE THEIR OWN LANGUAGE AND UNDERSTAND EACH OTHER. WE SEE THE PROOF OF IT IN THE FOLLOWING STORY, WHICH BEGINS IN THE SKIES OF ARMORICA, JUST ABOVE A LITTLE VILLAGE THAT WE KNOW WELL.

YOU'LL SOON HAVE EGG ALL OVER YOUR FACE, TITCH!
TCHAC!

NO BIRDS OF PREY IN MY POULTRY YARD!
PAF!
EEEEEK!

AND DON'T YOU SHOW YOUR NASTY BEAK IN HERE AGAIN, GET IT?
FLAP FLAP FLAP FLAP FLAP FLAP FLAP

THIS IS YOUR LUCKY DAY, MY YOUNG COCK-SPARROW, BUT I'M CHALLENGING YOU! TOMORROW AT DAWN, OUTSIDE THE VILLAGE, AND WE'LL SEE WHICH OF US IS THE BETTER EMBLEM.

YOU'RE NEVER GOING TO FACE THAT MONSTER, ARE YOU? HE'S MUCH STRONGER THAN YOU.
I KNOW, BUT I CAN'T BE CHICKEN ...

THE HONOUR OF ALL THE POULTRY YARDS OF GAUL IS AT STAKE!
2A

IF HE INSISTS, POOR CHANTICLEERIX WILL GET THE BIRD, THAT'S FOR SURE!

?!
BUT I KNOW SOMEONE WHO MIGHT BE ABLE TO HELP!
?!

HEY! DOGMATIX! ARE YOU AT HOME?
DOGMATIX

YES, WHAT DO YOU WANT, HENNA?
CHANTICLEERIX HAS ACCEPTED A CHALLENGE FROM THE IMPERIAL EAGLE! THEY'RE TO FIGHT A DUEL TOMORROW AT DAWN!
DOGMATIX
OH DEAR, I SEE! THAT BIRD WILL MAKE CHICKEN NUGGETS OF HIM!
UNLESS YOU CAN HELP. LISTEN, THIS IS MY IDEA ...
WHISPER WHISPER WHISPER ... RHUBARB ... WHISPER WHISPER ... SEE WHAT I MEAN?
HMMM, YES, BUT IT WON'T BE EASY!
NIGHT HAS FALLEN, AND EVERYONE IN THE VILLAGE IS ASLEEP. WELL, NOT QUITE EVERYONE ... ONE SMALL FOWL STILL HOLDS OUT AGAINST THE INVASION OF SLEEP.

OH DEAR ... YOU WON'T CATCH ME UP BEFORE THE BEAK AGAIN! OH HELP!
2B

AND NEXT MORNING AT DAWN ...
LET'S GO OUT IN THE FOREST AND PICK A FEW NICE BOARS FOR BREAKFAST.
OOH, YES! I LOVE PICKING THEM OFF WITH THE MORNING DEW STILL ON THEM!
DOGMATIX

THAT'S ODD, OBELIX. DOGMATIX HASN'T COME HUNTING WITH US!
YES, HE'LL BE BARKING MAD WHEN HE FINDS OUT!
DOGMATIX

DOGMATIX

WHAT LUCK! ASTERIX DIDN'T TAKE IT WITH HIM.

THE MAGIC POTION!!! YOU DID IT, DOGMATIX!
YOU DUMB CLUCK!
TCHRRRRR

WHERE'S CHANTICLEERIX?
FOLLOW ME! HE'S HIDING BEHIND THE HENHOUSE DOING PRESS-UPS!

DOGMATIX HAS BROUGHT YOU A SECRET WEAPON. YOU CAN DEFEAT YOUR IMPERIAL ENEMY WITH IT!
TWENTY-ONE, TWENTY-TWO ... WHAT IS IT? TWENTY-THREE, TWENTY ...
?!

MAGIC POTION!
!?

ER ... ARE YOU SURE POTION GOES WELL WITH CHICKEN?
DUNNO ... IT'V A RIVK YOU HAVE TO TAKE!

HEY... NO SKIVING OFF! THE VILLAGERS NEED THEIR ALARM CALL!
OKAY, OKAY ... COCKADOODLE DO! THAT DO YOU?

I'LL TAKE THE GOURD BACK BEFORE ASTERIX NOTICES THAT IT'S GONE!
GLUG! GLUG!

YOOHOOOOOO!

SEEMS TO BE WORKING!
YEF, IT FEEMF ...

?!
... TO BE FURKING!

OOH, ISN'T HE HANDSOME! AND HE'S FLYING!!
YEF, THAT'F NORMAL WHEN YOU'RE ON THE POTION! BYE NOW, HENNA!

I STILL DON'T SEE THAT GAULISH CHAMPION! HAS HE CHICKENED OUT?

TCHAC!

WH ... WHAT HAPPENED?
I'VE BEEN PLUCKED!

SPLATCH!

COCKADOODLE DO! AND I DID! COCKADOODLE-DOOO!

CLAP CLAP CLAP CLAP CLAP CLAP CLAP CLAP CLAP CLAP CLAP CLAP CLAP CLAP CLAP CLAP CLAP CLAP

- UDERZO - THE END

For Gaul Lang Syne
07 December 1967

Written by René Goscinny - Illustrated by Albert Uderzo

The issue of "Pilote" published at the end of the year always had to be about New Year customs...

This time René thought it would be a good idea if the Gauls joined in. He suggested to Albert reinventing an old custom dating back to Druid traditions: kissing under the mistletoe. In "Asterix the Legionary" Obelix fell in love with the beautiful Panacea, so the authors enjoyed going back to the subject. This time Obelix actually dares to try snatching a kiss, a very unusual situation for him ... but a skilful move thwarts his intentions. In condensed form, this story expresses all René Goscinny's delicacy of feeling and sense of humour, and the tender, beautiful line of Albert Uderzo's drawing.

"Pilote", n° 424

for Gaul Lang Syne

OBELIX!
PAF!

SMACK

YOU SHOULDN'T HAVE THUMPED THAT POOR ROMAN. A CUSTOM IS A CUSTOM!
?!?
O DRUID GETAFIX!

KISSY KISSY!
!

I'VE BROUGHT YOU SOME DRY WOOD, O DRUID!
OH, THERE YOU ARE, OBELIX!

YES! HERE I AM! THAT'S RIGHT, HERE I AM! NOW YOU SEE ME!

KISSY KISSY!

NOW YOU DON'T! THIS IS TOO MUCH! I'M KISSING OFF NOW, BY TOUTATIS!
?
?

WHAT'S THE MATTER, OBELIX? I WAS GOING TO TELL YOU I FOUND DOGMATIX AND HE ...
OH, THE LITTLE SCAMP!

SMACK!

THE END

Mini Midi Maxi
02 August 1971

Written by René Goscinny - Illustrated by Albert Uderzo

In view of the huge success of Asterix and his friends, the weekly magazine "Elle" asked the authors to provide a story on a women's subject for one of their summer issues.

Although it is true that the village of indomitable Gauls is rather a male society, the authors progressively introduced heroines into the story as regular characters, for instance Impedimenta the chief's wife, Mrs Geriatrix (the star of this two-page story), Panacea and Cleopatra.

So it would be wrong to call the authors of the Asterix books anti-feminist! In fact women play a much more important part than in many other famous series! And if the humour sometimes gently mocks them, it certainly doesn't spare the men either. Look at the rather unflattering pictures of Chief Vitalstatistix, Unhygienix the fishmonger or Fulliautomatix the village blacksmith! Thank you!

"Elle" n° 1337

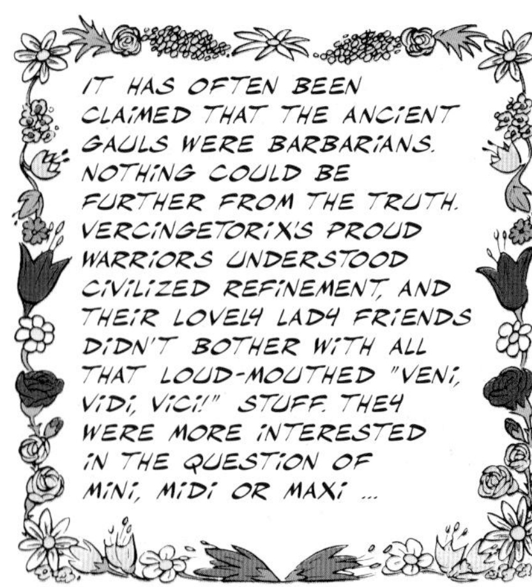
IT HAS OFTEN BEEN CLAIMED THAT THE ANCIENT GAULS WERE BARBARIANS. NOTHING COULD BE FURTHER FROM THE TRUTH. VERCINGETORIX'S PROUD WARRIORS UNDERSTOOD CIVILIZED REFINEMENT, AND THEIR LOVELY LADY FRIENDS DIDN'T BOTHER WITH ALL THAT LOUD-MOUTHED "VENI, VIDI, VICI!" STUFF. THEY WERE MORE INTERESTED IN THE QUESTION OF MINI, MIDI OR MAXI ...

FOR INSTANCE, TAKE THIS CHARMING GAULISH LADY ...

OR NO ... LET'S TAKE THIS ONE!

NOTICE THE NATURAL ELEGANCE OF HER FIGURE ...

... AND THE INFINITE CARE SHE HAS TAKEN WITH HER HAIRSTYLE.
I'M A CELEBRITY! GET ME BACK IN THERE!

AND NOW TO STUDY GAULISH FASHIONS ...
I MEAN, I AM THE CHIEF'S WIFE!

GAULISH WOMEN WORE A TUNIC ...
LOOK, IMPEDIMENTA, WOULD YOU MIND LEAVING US ALONE? CAN'T YOU SEE WE'RE BUSY?
WHAT WAS THAT?

SOMETIMES WITH A SECOND TUNIC WORN OVER IT ...
YOU LITTLE MADAM! WHO SAYS YOU CAN TALK TO ME LIKE THAT?
GERIATRIX, SWEETIE!

... IN AN ELEGANTLY MATCHING COLOUR.
WHAT'S THE MATTER, POPSY?
POPSY HERE IS A PROPER LITTLE MADAM, THAT'S WHAT!

THE CLOSE-FITTING ATTRACTIVELY LOW-CUT BODICE ...
GERIATRIX, HONEYBUN, ARE YOU GOING TO LET HER SAY THOSE THINGS?
WELL ... ER ... NO ... LISTEN, IMPEDIMENTA ...
VITALSTATISTIX!

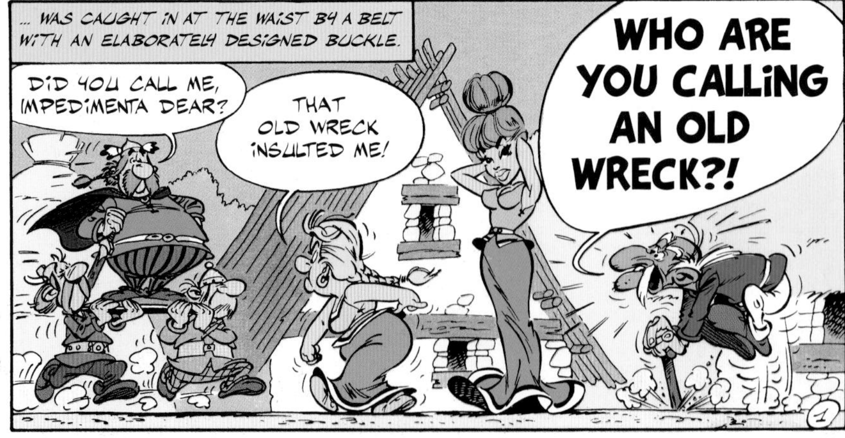
... WAS CAUGHT IN AT THE WAIST BY A BELT WITH AN ELABORATELY DESIGNED BUCKLE.
DID YOU CALL ME, IMPEDIMENTA DEAR?
THAT OLD WRECK INSULTED ME!
WHO ARE YOU CALLING AN OLD WRECK?!
1

THE GAULISH WOMAN OFTEN WEARS DRAPERY IN THE ROMAN STYLE, THUS ADDING AN ARISTOCRATIC TOUCH TO HER OUTFIT.
GET DOWN OFF THERE IF YOU'RE A MAN!
WHAT?!
WHAT'S ALL THIS SHOUTING ABOUT?
THIS LITTLE MADAM TOOK MY PLACE ...

LET US ALSO ADMIRE HER JEWELLERY ...
HAS-BEEN! FOSSIL! DILAPIDATED OLD CODGER!
WANT TO FEEL THE WRONG END OF MY STICK?
TELL ME HONESTLY, BACTERIA, DO YOU THINK SHE'S PRETTIER THAN ME?
YES.

... WHICH IS ALWAYS IN EXQUISITE TASTE.
UNHYGIENIX!
?!

IT IS MADE OF METAL, BONE OR GLASS ...
WHAT BUSINESS IS IT OF YOURS, YOU GREAT GOOF?
CALM DOWN, CALM DOWN!

ELEGANT GAULISH LADIES LOVE NECKLACES, BRACELETS AND BROOCHES ...
EVEN THE CHIEF HAS NO RIGHT TO CALL ME A GREAT GOOF!
SPLATCH!

... WHICH ARE MASTERPIECES OF BEAUTY AND DISTINCTION.
COME ON, QUICK, OBELIX! THERE'S A PUNCH-UP GOING ON!
GOODY!

THE GAULISH LADY TAKES GREAT CARE WITH HER MAKE-UP ...
I'M THE CHIEF AROUND HERE AND I CAN CALL ANYONE I LIKE A GREAT GOOF!
SPLOTCH!
I DUCKED! I DUCKED! YAH BOO SUCKS TO YOU!

ALL THIS MAKES THE GAULISH LADY A DAINTY, ADORABLE CREATURE ...

... SYMBOLIZING THE REFINEMENT OF THOSE WHOM HISTORIANS HAVE UNTHINKINGLY DESCRIBED AS BARBARIANS.
THE END
2
-UDERZO- & GOSCINNY

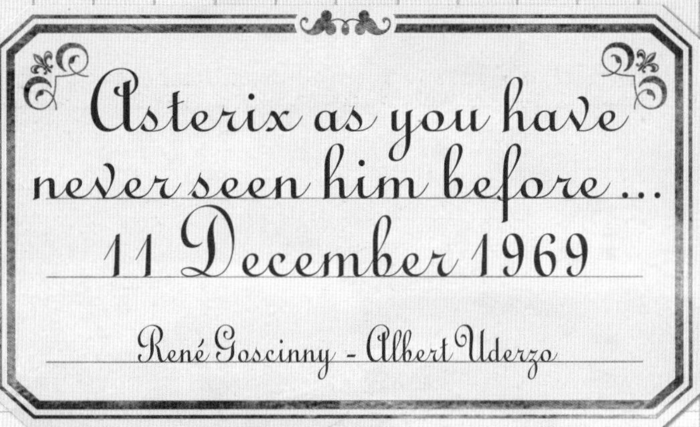

Asterix as you have never seen him before...
11 December 1969
René Goscinny - Albert Uderzo

These three pages of anthology pieces, which have kept all their force and originality, are very much in the spirit of "Pilote" magazine in the 1960s. The texts make their points tellingly and are very funny, while the drawing — or rather drawings — show a breathtaking mastery of many different graphic styles. How can an artist change his own style to caricature other strip cartoon illustrators so cleverly? There is a touch of the famous American "Mad" magazine here. The author has fun showing us what his imagination has come up with — for by agreement with René Goscinny, Albert both wrote and drew these three amazing pages by himself. A treat to be (re)discovered.

"Pilote", n° 527

SINCE THE BIRTH OF ASTERIX, MANY OF OUR READERS AND CERTAIN SPECIALIST STRIP CARTOON MAGAZINES, NOT TO MENTION THE CRITICS, HAVE SUGGESTED IDEAS TO US. WE WOULD LIKE TO THANK THEM FOR THEIR KIND CONTRIBUTIONS, AND WE THOUGHT IT WOULD BE INTERESTING TO ADAPT ASTERIX IN LINE WITH SOME OF THEIR SUGGESTIONS.

SUGGESTION 1

"WHY DON'T YOU, LIKE, YOU KNOW, HAVE THE DRUID INVENTING MODERN GADGETS? THE CHARACTERS DON'T TALK, LIKE, NATURAL. AND EVEN WORSE, THE DRAWING'S JUST FOR KIDS, LIKE MICKEY MOUSE STUFF. SIGNED, A PAL."

SUGGESTION 2

"'STORIES TOO LONG' - STOP - 'TOO MUCH DIALOGUE' - STOP - 'NOT ENOUGH SIMPLICITY IN DRAWING' - STOP - 'WHY NOT TAKE ASTERIX TO AMERICA?' - STOP - SIGNED, PROFESSOR HEDDY, UNIVERSITY OF NANTES."

SUGGESTION 3

"THE LATEST ASTERIX BOOK WAS NOT TOO BAD, UNATTRACTIVE AND MUDDLED AS THE DRAWING WAS. ON THE OTHER HAND WE WERE DELIGHTED TO RE-READ THE WONDERFUL COLLECTION OF THE ADVENTURES OF THE HIGH-FLYING CRASH CORDON IN THE AMAZING WORLD OF DEEP SPACE."

FROM A REVIEW IN "PHOEBUS", THE JOURNAL OF ASCII (ASSOCIATION FOR STRIP CARTOON INFORMATION INTERCHANGE)

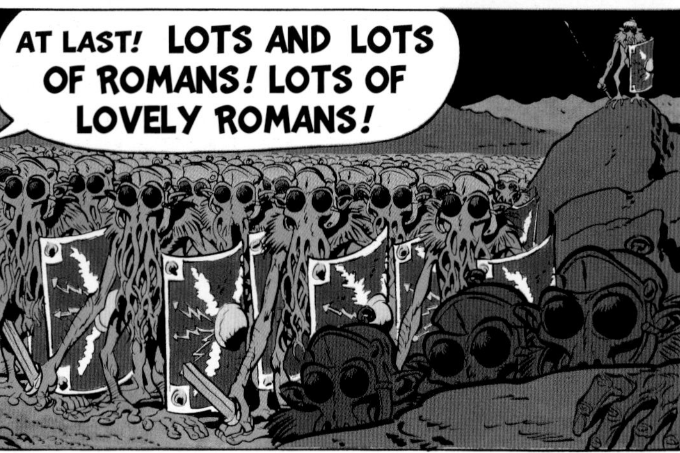

SUGGESTION 4 *"I AM A SYCOPHANT AIMING TO PROMOTE CINEDOLOGICALLY NECROMANTIC SYMBIOSIS. MY EGO REBELS AGAINST YOUR WORK AND URGES DEHORTATION. THE CRETINOIDAL MICROCEPHALY OF YOUR PHYLACTERIO-LOGICAL TEXT, TOGETHER WITH THE MONSTROUS SPACIOSITY OF EMPIRICIST GRAPHICS SUGGESTING RETROSPECTIVE DELIRIUM, IS AN INSULT TO THE INTELLECT AND TO THE STUDY OF UNIVERSALS AS ENVISAGED AND CARRIED OUT BY THE MIND." HUBERT BLETHER, EDITOR, "THE LITERARY SYCOPHANT". (AUTHORS' NOTE: THIS SUGGESTION IS OBVIOUSLY FOR A WEIGHTIER AND MORE INTELLECTUAL TEXT.)*

YOU SAY A GREAT MANY THINGS IN ATTEMPTING TO SEEM TO CONTRADICT ME, YET NONETHELESS YOU SAY NOTHING THAT CONTRADICTS ME SINCE YOU COME TO THE SAME CONCLUSION AS I DO. NONETHELESS YOU INTERPOSE IN CERTAIN PASSAGES SEVERAL REMARKS TO WHICH I CANNOT AGREE, FOR INSTANCE THAT THE AXIOM *THERE IS NOTHING IN AN EFFECT WHICH WAS NOT PREVIOUSLY IN ITS CAUSE* SHOULD BE UNDERSTOOD AS DENOTING THE MATERIAL CAUSE RATHER THAN THE EFFICACY, FOR IT IS IMPOSSIBLE TO CONCEIVE OF PERFECTION OF FORM PRE-EXISTING IN THE MATERIAL CAUSE, ONLY IN THE SOLE EFFICACIOUS CAUSE, AND ALSO YOU SAY THAT ...

... THE FORMAL REALITY OF AN IDEA IS A SUBSTANCE, WITH SEVERAL OTHER SIMILAR REMARKS. IF YOU HAD ANY EVIDENCE OF THE EXISTENCE OF MATERIAL THINGS THEN NO DOUBT YOU WOULD HAVE SET IT DOWN HERE. BUT SINCE YOU ASK ONLY, "IF IT IS THEREFORE TRUE THAT I AM NOT CERTAIN OF THE EXISTENCE OF ANYTHING BESIDES MYSELF IN THE WORLD," AND SINCE YOU PRETEND THERE IS NO NEED TO LOOK FOR REASONS FOR SOMETHING SO OBVIOUS, AND THUS YOU ARE REPORTING ONLY YOUR OLD PREJUDICES, YOU MAKE IT ALL THE MORE CLEAR THAT YOU HAVE NO REASONS ...

... PROVING WHAT YOU SAY, ANY MORE THAN IF YOU HAD NEVER SAID ANYTHING AT ALL. AS FOR WHAT YOU SAY ABOUT IDEAS, IT NEEDS NO REPLY BECAUSE YOU CONFINE THE TERM OF IDEA SOLELY TO IMAGES DEPICTED IN THE IMAGINATION, WHILE I UNDERSTAND IT AS ALL THAT WE CONCEIVE OF IN OUR THOUGHTS. HOWEVER, I WILL ASK, IN PASSING, WHAT ARGUMENT YOU CITE TO PROVE THAT "NOTHING ACTS UPON ITSELF", FOR IT IS NOT YOUR HABIT TO USE ARGUMENTS IN EVIDENCE OF WHAT YOU SAY. YOU MAY SAY YOU PROVE IT BY THE EXAMPLE OF THE FINGER WHICH CANNOT STRIKE ITSELF, AND THE EYE WHICH CANNOT SEE ITSELF EXCEPT IN A MIRROR, TO WHICH IT IS EASY TO REPLY THAT IT IS BY NO MEANS THE EYE WHICH SEES ITSELF OR THE MIRROR, BUT THE MIND, WHICH ALONE KNOWS BOTH THE MIRROR AND THE EYE AND ITSELF. ONE MAY EVEN CITE FURTHER EXAMPLES DRAWN FROM CORPOREAL MATTERS CONCERNING THE ACTION A THING MAY HAVE UPON ITSELF, AS WHEN A CURVED PLANE TURNS IN UPON ITSELF, FOR IS NOT THAT CONVERSION AN ACTION EXERCISED UPON ITSELF?*

* REPLIES TO OBJECTION V TO THE MEDITATIONS OF DESCARTES.

SUGGESTION 5 "I'D LIKE TO SEE ASTERIX A BIT MORE TRENDY, A PSYCHEDELIX ASTERIX, FOR INSTANCE! AND WHY DON'T WOMEN FEATURE MORE IN YOUR STORIES? YOU'RE NOT ANTI-FEMINISTS, ARE YOU? AVE, FRIENDS! SIGNED: A FAN."

THANKS TO THE DRUID'S MAGIC FLOWERS, WE CAN NOW DO A PROPER JOB OF FIGHTING THE WILD WOMEN WARRIORS LED BY PROCONSULESS DEODORA, OBELIX!

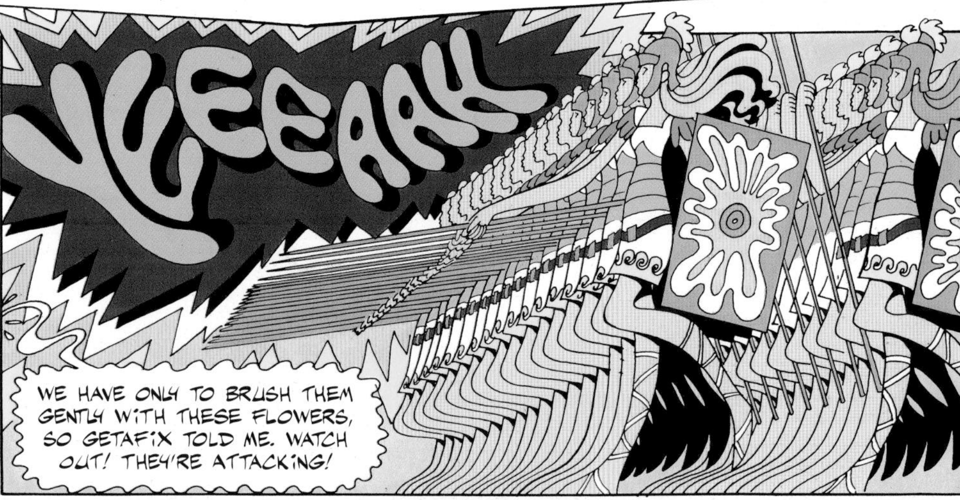
YEEARK
WE HAVE ONLY TO BRUSH THEM GENTLY WITH THESE FLOWERS, SO GETAFIX TOLD ME. WATCH OUT! THEY'RE ATTACKING!

TCHIC

IF YOU ASK ME, ASTERIX, THIS ISN'T AS MUCH FUN AS A GOOD PUNCH-UP!

AND HERE IS THE LAST SUGGESTION, THE ONE WHICH WE, AS THE AUTHORS, WOULD LIKE TO PUT TO YOU, OUR READERS. IT'S A QUESTION OF AESTHETICS, WHICH JUST SUDDENLY CAME TO US. A DARING IDEA, WE ADMIT, BUT ALL THE SAME WE KNOW OUR CHARACTERS WELL, I MEAN WE MADE THEM UP, DIDN'T WE? SO WE HAVE A RIGHT TO HAVE IDEAS TOO, OH YES WE DO! OH, REALLY, WE DON'T BELIEVE IT!?! **SHUT UP! WE'RE FREE AGENTS, AREN'T WE? VERY WELL, IF THAT'S HOW YOU LOT FEEL, IN FUTURE ASTERIX AND OBELIX WILL WEAR PLUS-FOURS...**

HONESTLY! I MEAN, I ASK YOU! THESE AUTHORS ARE CRAZY!
TAP! TAP! TAP!
TAP! TAP! TAP!
UDERZO

The Lutetia Olympics
25 October 1986
Written and illustrated by Albert Uderzo

In the mid-1980s the mayor of Paris turned to Asterix for help in its Olympic bid. Jacques Chirac and his municipal team wanted Paris (the former city of Lutetia) to stage the AD 1992 Games.

Albert Uderzo was asked to create a poster and a small four-page strip cartoon story to win support from the Parisii tribe of Lutetia. He liked the idea, and designed a poster which went up all over the capital in 1986. The story was published in "Jours de France", a popular magazine of the last century.

In the end the Olympic Committee did not award the Games to Paris, but obviously not everyone lost out, since just for the record, the original of the poster was never returned to the artist! But never mind: here you can see the Eiffel Tower turned into a huge, magnificent dovecote, and a really nasty villain is added to the rogues' gallery of the Asterix stories.

VIVE PARIS CAPITALE OLYMPIQUE MCMXCII*

PARIS 1992

UDERZO

"Jours de France", n° 1660

* 1992

"EXACTLY 100 YEARS AGO A GAULISH ATHLETE CALLED PIERRE DECOUBERTIX WON AT THE OLYMPIC GAMES IN GREECE. IT WAS THE FIRST TIME A NON-GREEK ATHLETE HAD EVER BEEN CROWNED WITH THE LAUREL WREATH OF VICTORY. TO COMMEMORATE THIS EVENT, THE OLYMPIC COMMITTEE HAS DECIDED TO HOLD ITS NEXT GAMES OUTSIDE GREECE!"

PFFFFF!

"ROME HAS ALSO MADE A BID FOR THE GAMES. JULIUS CAESAR IS SURE TO CAUSE TROUBLE TO ENSURE THAT ROME GETS CHOSEN. SO I AM ASKING THE VILLAGE OF INDOMITABLE GAULS TO HELP US. PLEASE SEND YOUR MOST COURAGEOUS WARRIORS! THE HONOUR OF GAUL IS AT STAKE!"

AND OUR FRIENDS SET OFF FOR LUTETIA.
LET ME DOWN AGAIN AND I'LL BE THE ONE DROPPING YOU. YOU'LL BE SACKED, SEE?

AT THE SAME TIME, IN ROME ...
INGLORIUS PITHECANTHROPUS, YOU'RE HEAD OF MY SECRET SERVICE. I AM ENTRUSTING A VERY DELICATE MISSION TO YOU. YOU START FOR LUTETIA AT ONCE!

ONCE IN LUTETIA, YOU WILL SPY ON THE OLYMPIC COMMITTEE VISITING THE CELTIC CAPITAL. IF YOU DETECT THE SLIGHTEST HINT OF SATISFACTION ON THEIR PART, THE LEAST TRACE OF A FAVOURABLE OPINION, YOU HAVE MY PERMISSION TO ACT!

FOR ONLY ROME MUST BE RECOGNIZED AS THE OLYMPIC CAPITAL!
YOUR WORD IS MY COMMAND, GREAT CAESAR!
PAF!

AFTER SEVERAL DAYS ON THE ROAD OUR HEROES ARRIVE IN LUTETIA, THE CITY OF LIGHT.
WE'RE THE INDOMITABLE GAULS WHO ...
YES, I WAS EXPECTING YOU. MY NAME IS CIVILSERVIX, AND I AM PERMANENT SECRETARY TO PARTIPOLITIX, WHO ASKS YOU TO EXCUSE HIM. HE'S BUSY DEBATING VARIOUS PROBLEMS WITH OTHER TRIBAL CHIEFTAINS!
GAULISH HOUSES OF PARLIAMENT

COME WITH ME! I WAS JUST ABOUT TO WELCOME THE OLYMPICCOMMITTEE. THEY'RE ARRIVING BY R.E.R.
WHAT ARIA?

REGIONAL EUROSTELLA ROUTES!
?!
RER

AS YOU SEE, LUTETIA IS AT THE CUTTING EDGE OF NEW TECHNOLOGY!!
YEAH.

IF YOU'LL BE KIND ENOUGH TO FOLLOW ME, I'LL SHOW YOU ROUND ...

... OUR GREAT CITY OF ART AND LITERATURE!
YEAH.
DOGMATIX SEEMS TO HAVE SMELT A RAT!
BETTER KEEP OUR EYES OPEN.
GRRRRR

THE HIGH CULTURAL REPUTATION OF LUTETIA MAKES IT THE CROSSROADS OF THE ANCIENT WORLD.
YEAH.

LUTETIA IS ALSO FAMOUS FOR THE WARMTH OF ITS WELCOME, ITS HOTELS AND ITS FINE FOOD!
YEAH.
OH, ASTERIX, I'M HUNGRY!
3A

THIS IS THE CARRIER PIGEON TOWER, WHICH HAS GIVEN LUTETIA A REPUTATION FOR RUNNING THE FASTEST COMMUNICATIONS SYSTEM IN THE ANCIENT WORLD...
YEAH.

... WITH ONLY THE OCCASIONAL FOWL-UP.
OH YEAH?

HERE ARE THE LUTETIAN ARENAS, SITUATED CLOSE TO THE HEART OF THE CITY AND ABLE TO HOLD THE MAXIMUM NUMBER OF SPECTATORS. ALL THE OLYMPIC SPORTS CAN BE STAGED HERE!
YEAH.
I HAVE A CUNNING PLAN! LET'S KIDNAP THE PRESIDENT OF THE OLYMPIC COMMITTEE! LUTETIA WILL BE DISGRACED AND LOSE ANY CHANCE OF BEING PICKED FOR THE GAMES. TEEHEEHEE!
3B

WE DON'T WANT YOUR OLYMPIC GAMES IN LUTETIA, AND YOU DON'T GET YOUR PRESIDENT BACK UNTIL YOU LEAVE THE COUNTRY FOR GOOD. GREEKS GO HOME!
TIME WE STEPPED IN, OBELIX!
OH, YEAH, ASTERIX!
GLUG! GLUG! GLUG!
GRRRR!

PIF!
PAF!

SOON AFTERWARDS ...
I HOPE WE DIDN'T ALARM YOU! THAT WAS JUST A LITTLE EXERCISE TO DEMONSTRATE THE EFFICIENCY OF OUR SECURITY SERVICE!
4A

THAT WAS FAN-TAS-TIC!
?

LUTETIA SHALL BE THE NEXT OLYMPIC CAPITAL!! THE EFFICIENCY OF YOUR SECURITY SERVICE HAS WON YOU THE GAMES!
OH, IT WAS ONLY A ROUTINE EXERCISE!

PHEW ... WHAT WOULD IT HAF BEEN LIKE FOR WEAL?

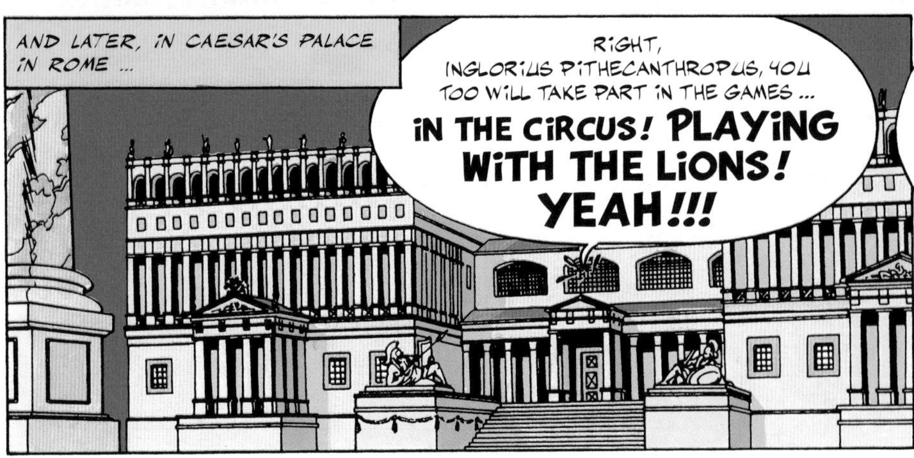
AND LATER, IN CAESAR'S PALACE IN ROME ...
RIGHT, INGLORIUS PITHECANTHROPUS, YOU TOO WILL TAKE PART IN THE GAMES ... IN THE CIRCUS! PLAYING WITH THE LIONS! YEAH!!!
AFTER THE SUCCESS OF THE LUTETIA GAMES, TOUTATIS TELLS ME THAT THE PARISII OF THE FUTURE WILL BE STAGING ANOTHER OLYMPIC GAMES IN THEIR BEAUTIFUL CITY TOO!
4B
7-86-
UDERZO

Springtime in Gaul
17 March 1966

René Goscinny - Albert Uderzo

René Goscinny, overworked at the time, asked Albert if he had any ideas for a story about spring. For the second time Albert wrote a little story of his own and showed it to his colleague before he drew the pictures.

René was delighted with the magical seasons, so Albert created this two-page story on his own, as well as the cover picture of the magazine. Albert was inspired by his childhood, when he loved walking from the Faubourg Saint-Antoine to Aligre market near the Bastille in Paris, where the costermongers sold fruit and vegetables from their barrows.

René simply suggested to his friend the part played by Obelix in the final delightful gag.

"Pilote", n° 334

Springtime in Gaul
SPRING'S A LONG TIME COMING! STILL NO BOARS TO HUNT, NO OTHER GAME ...
NO ROMANS GAME FOR A FIGHT EITHER. I'M FED UP!
GOSCINNY
UDERZO

LOOK, OBELIX!!!

A LITTLE MAN IN A BAD WAY!!!
JUDGING BY HIS SIZE, IT'S A LONG TIME SINCE HE WAS FED UP!

LET'S TAKE HIM TO GETAFIX. OUR DRUID WILL BE ABLE TO CURE HIM ...
IT WOULD BE HANDY IF WE COULD CALL A MOBILE DRUID.
1A

AND A LITTLE LATER, THANKS TO THE EXPERT CARE OF GETAFIX THE DRUID ...
I'VE NEVER SEEN ANYTHING LIKE IT!
WHO ARE YOU, O LITTLE MAN?
YOU THINK THESE LITTLE THINGIES CAN TALK?

OF COURSE THEY CAN. EVERY BIT AS WELL AS THOSE BIG FAT THINGIES! I AM SPRING!

... FAVOURITE SON OF THE GREAT BARROW-GIRL IN THE SKY WHO SENDS SEASONAL PRODUCE DOWN TO EARTH!
WATCH OUT, SON! WINTER'S BEEN PARTICULARLY HARD THIS YEAR!
DON'T WORRY, BY TOUTATIS! I SHALL DEFEAT HIM, SAME AS USUAL!
Springtime Novelties

FULL OF CONFIDENCE, I DROPPED TO EARTH ...
HERE I COME! WE'LL SEE WHO'S THE MOST SEASONED FIGHTER!

WHERE ARE YOU, WINTER? I'M GOING TO MAKE IT HOT FOR YOU!
TEEHEE! DON'T LOSE YOUR COOL!

BANG!
1B

TEEHEEHEE! AND NOW TO SPREAD A FLU EPIDEMIC THROUGH THE WHOLE ANCIENT WORLD!

WHO'S A BIG FAT THING?
OH, LEAVE IT OUT, OBELIX! WE MUST DO SOMETHING TO HELP SPRING.
MAGIC POTION! YOU TWO BRING ME MY BIG CAULDRON!

AND A LITTLE LATER ...
DRINK THIS!

FLYING LIKE A SWALLOW!
THANKS!

ONE SWALLOW MAKES ME SPRING ... IT'S BACK TO WINTER QUARTERS FOR YOU!
?
!?!

NO MORE MR ICE GUY!
TCHAC!

SPRING HAS SPRUNG! HAVING PUT WINTER TO FLIGHT FOR MANY MONTHS, HE HAPPILY GETS DOWN TO WORK ...

WHEREVER HE GOES BUDS OPEN, GRASS GROWS, AND EVERYTHING IN SIGHT IS FULL OF THE JOYS OF SPRING!
!?!

AND WITH SUNSHINE AND SPRING SHOWERS, THAT SPRINGTIME IN GAUL IS THE BEST EVER!
BY JUPITER, THESE GAULS ARE A SHOWER!
ASTERIX, I'BE GOT HAY FEBER ... DO YOU THINK A LITTLE BAGIC POTION WOULD ... ?
BANG! BANG! BANG!
THE END

The mascot
13 June 1968

Written by René Goscinny - Illustrated by Albert Uderzo

The story of "The mascot" was originally published in the smaller format of the "Super Pocket Pilote" series, and in a magazine commissioned by the town council of Romainville – one of the suburbs of Lutetia. With a name like that – "Roman-town" – it was not surprising that the council should invite Asterix and his friends to pay a visit. In this complete story, full of the familiar features of the Asterix adventures, Dogmatix is kidnapped. Obelix's little friend, who first appeared in "Asterix and the Banquet", soon became one of the favourite characters in the village. Here he is the victim of his own charms – after all, anyone would want a little dog who was so keen on preserving the environment twenty centuries ahead of his time!

It was all thanks to Dogmatix that Obelix stopped uprooting trees and became ecologixally conscious!

"Super Pocket Pilote", n°1

the mascot
TEXT BY
GOSCINNY
DRAWN BY
-UDERZO-

ABSOLUTELY, ASTERIX! I TELL YOU DOGMATIX IS A GREAT LITTLE DOG! THE TROUBLE IS YOU DON'T TRUST HIM. IT GIVES HIM AN INFERIORITY COMPLEX!*
NEVER MIND THAT. LOOK WHO'S HERE!
* THE ORIGIN OF THE MODERN COMPLEX.

WHO SHOULD BE HERE BUT A FINE UPSTANDING ROMAN PATROL?
TWO GAULS!
NOT THE TWO GAULS?!
DULCE ET DECORUM EST PRO PATRIA MORI.
SHUT UP, IGNORAMUS!

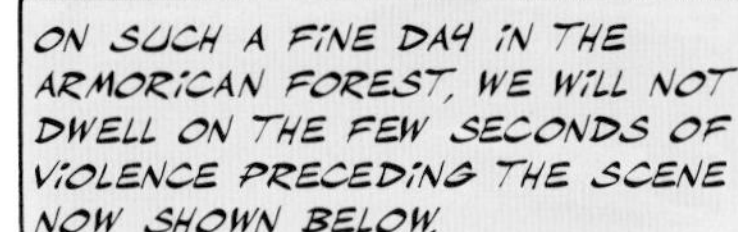
ON SUCH A FINE DAY IN THE ARMORICAN FOREST, WE WILL NOT DWELL ON THE FEW SECONDS OF VIOLENCE PRECEDING THE SCENE NOW SHOWN BELOW.

HONESTLY, THEY'RE GOING TOO FAR!
WE DIDN'T DO A THING TO THOSE CHAUVINIST GAULISH BOORS! ALL WE DID WAS INVADE THEM!
VICTRIX CAUSA DIIS PLACUIT, SED VICTA CATONI!
IF YOU'RE QUITE THROUGH WITH THE CLASSICAL QUOTATIONS ...

NUNC EST BIBENDUM.
ALL THAT FOREST TO PATROL AND WE HAVE TO RUN INTO THOSE SOCIAL MISFITS! WE'RE DOWN ON OUR LUCK!
OH, LEAVE IT OUT!
YOU KNOW WHY WE'RE DOWN ON OUR LUCK?
1

WHY?
CUR, QUID, QUOMODO?
YOU'RE BEGINNING TO GET ME DOWN, YOU ARE!
BECAUSE WE DON'T HAVE A MASCOT!

A MASCOT?
OF COURSE! WE NEED A MASCOT! OUR MATES BACK HOME ON THE CAPITOL HAVE THE SACRED GEESE. THOSE GEESE TURNED OUT GOOD EGGS!
RES, NON VERBA.
YOU ASKED FOR IT!

HE'S GOT A RIGHT TO SPEAK LATIN GRAMMAR!
JUST WATCH HIM PARSING THROUGH!
I'M GOING TO LOOK FOR A LITTLE ANIMAL TO BE OUR MASCOT!
PAF!

I'M SURE TO FIND A LITTLE ANIMAL SOMEWHERE IN THIS FOREST.

AT THAT VERY MOMENT...
WATCH THIS! THEN YOU'LL SEE WHAT A GREAT LITTLE DOG MY DOGMATIX IS!
WHAT DO YOU EXPECT YOUR GREAT LITTLE DOGMATIX TO DO?

FETCH, DOGMATIX!
2

TCHOK!

WOOF?

HEY, HERE'S OUR MASCOT!
?

A STUNNING STROKE OF LUCK! ALL OUR TROUBLES ARE OVER!
GRRRR!

LOOK, BOYS! OUR LUCKY MASCOT! WHEN I SAW HIM INSPIRATION STRUCK!
BEFORE OR AFTER YOU SAW HIM, WAS IT?

MEANWHILE ...
DOGMATIX ISN'T BACK YET ... THAT'S FUNNY.
I KNEW THAT MENHIR WAS TOO BIG FOR HIM!

YOU JUST DON'T TRUST DOGMATIX! OF COURSE, HE'S NOT VERY SELF-CONFIDENT YET!
NEVER MIND ARGUING, LET'S LOOK FOR HIM!

THERE'S THE MENHIR!
YES, BUT WHERE'S DOGMATIX?

HE MUST BE PLAYING WITH THE PRETTY BUTTERFLIES ... DOGMATIX LIKES BUTTERFLIES. DOGMATIX ... DOGMATIX!
YOOHOO! DOGMATIX!
OBELIX, LOOK AT THAT!

A ROMAN LEGIONARY'S HELMET!!!

A HELMET? BUT DOGMATIX AND THE MENHIR WERE BOTH BARE-HEADED WHEN ...
DON'T YOU SEE, OBELIX? A LEGIONARY HAS KIDNAPPED DOGMATIX!!!

KIDNAPPED DOGMATIX? I'LL TEACH THEM TO GO KIDNAPPING DOGMATIX! BY TOUTATIS, I WILL!
CALM DOWN, DO, OBELIX!

I DON'T WANT TO CALM DOWN! I WANT DOGMATIX!!!
LET ME JUST TAKE A LITTLE MAGIC POTION AND WE'LL BE OFF, OBELIX!

MEANWHILE ...
WHAT SHALL WE CALL OUR MASCOT?
SOMETHING TO REMIND US OF HOME ...
SOMETHING ENDING IN "US"...
HERE'S A NICE BONUS FOR HIM ANYWAY!
GRRRRR

WHAT HAVE YOU GOT THERE, MEN?
A MASCOT, CENTURION!
SCRUNCH SCRUNCH

VERY SWEET ... BUT HE DOESN'T LOOK VERY OBEDIENT ... I'LL TRAIN HIM FOR YOU, BY JUPITER!
GRRRRRR!

WOOF! WOOF!
AHA! YOU WON'T TRY BITING ME AGAIN, EH? YOU RECOGNIZE YOUR MASTER!
ER ... I THINK HE DOES ...

!?!
5

WHO LET THESE GAULS INTO CAMP, AND WHAT DO THEY WANT?

HE LET US INTO CAMP ...
... AND WE WANT DOGMATIX!

LET THAT SENTRY GO, AND AS FOR THE DOG, COME AND GET HIM, BY MERCURY!

THERE HE GOES ...
... AND HERE WE COME, BY TOUTATIS!

6
TCHAC!
PAF!
TCHOC!
SCRUNCH! SCRUNCH!

THAT'S ENOUGH FUN, DOGMATIX. WE'RE OFF.
AND DON'T LET US CATCH YOU DOING IT AGAIN, BY BELENOS!
LICK!

...OOOOOOH!

SO WE THINK A MASCOT IS A GOOD IDEA, DO WE? SO WE'RE LOOKING AT OUR CENTURION WITH SUBTLE IRONY, ARE WE?
?
?
?

RIGHT, OFF YOU GO TO PATROL THE FOREST AGAIN, JUST TO TEACH YOU A LESSON! QUICK MARCH!

OH, WHAT A BRILLIANT IDEA! THAT MASCOT CERTAINLY BROUGHT US LUCK!
HOW WAS I TO KNOW?
BEATI PAUPERES SPIRITU!
YOU COULD SHOW SOME SPIRIT TOO!
7

WATCH OUT!
CLING!
CLANG!
CLONG!

THE LUCKY MASCOT! RUN FOR YOUR LIVES!!!

WOOF! WOOF!
SEE HOW MUCH MORE SELF-CONFIDENT DOGMATIX IS SINCE THE ROMANS TRUSTED HIM, ASTERIX?
I MUST ADMIT THAT FOR ONCE, OBELIX, YOU ARE ABSOLUTELY RIGHT!
THE END
8

Latinomania
March 1973

Written by René Goscinny - Illustrated by Albert Uderzo

Thirty years ago, amused by the campaign against the use of English words in French — a phenomenon known as "franglais" — René Goscinny decided to use the Gauls to poke fun at it. He replied indirectly and humorously to the famous author Maurice Druon, one of the keenest to defend the purity of French, by imagining a similar fashion for "Latinisms" in occupied Gaul, and wrote this story, drawn by Albert Uderzo. It will certainly teach you more Latin than the other stories in this collection, by Toutatis!

This story, entitled "Latinomania" or "Et cetera", has been completely re-inked and re-coloured, like most of the stories here that date from the 1960s. Below is the cover of the first edition of the book you are now reading, published in France in 1993. Four hundred thousand copies were sold within weeks. However, it has never before been published in English, so all fourteen stories are new to readers of Asterix on the other side of the Channel.

Astérix et la rentrée gauloise
Dix histoires courtes
Textes René GOSCINNY
Dessins Albert UDERZO
La table de multiplication
V x I = V
V x II = X
LES EDITIONS ALBERT RENÉ

Just for the record, on 10 August 1993, the day the first edition (in a giftbox with the videos of the first Asterix films) was released, the French publishers' switchboards crashed. The success of the book, which sold far more copies than the most optimistic had expected, persuaded us to promise a new, improved and longer edition to the readers and booksellers who have been waiting eagerly for it. Would we ever give in to blackmail? By Toutatis, no! But here at last is the book!

BACK IN THE 60s A NUMBER OF ENGLISH WORDS INVADED THE FRENCH LANGUAGE. THE RESULT WAS KNOWN AS FRANGLAIS. BUT IT WAS NOT THE FIRST TIME SUCH A THING HAD HAPPENED. IN ANCIENT GAUL BACK IN THE 60s (BC, OF COURSE) ...

HEY, YOU TWO! KEEP OFF MY GERANIUMS!
OOPS! MEA CULPA!

YOU MIGHT PAY A MINIMUM OF ATTENTION!
A LITTLE DECORUM, PLEASE, DEAR!

THERE'S NO NEED TO SHOUT! THIS ISN'T A FORUM OR AN AUDITORIUM!
ME, SHOUTING? IT'S YOU SHOUTING! SHUT UP, AND THAT'S AN ULTIMATUM!

ULTIMATUM? WE'LL SEE ABOUT THAT!
NO! NOT THE AQUARIUM!

I HEARD ALL THAT! IT'S A CRYING SHAME. SPEAKING LATIN! WE MUST PRESERVE THE PURITY OF OUR BEAUTIFUL GAULISH LANGUAGE!
SPEAKING LATIN? US?
GLUG GLUGGLUG GLUG GLUG?

THAT'S RIGHT. AUDITORIUM, ULTIMATUM, AQUARIUM: THEY'RE ALL LATIN WORDS!
BUT WHAT OUGHT WE TO SAY INSTEAD, O DRUID?

WELL, "HALL FOR PUBLIC PERFORMANCES", "FINAL DEMAND ALLOWING NO ARGUMENT", "GLASS CONTAINER FOR FRESH-WATER OR SALT-WATER FISH" ...

ETCETERA, ETCETERA.
UDERZO & GOSCINNY

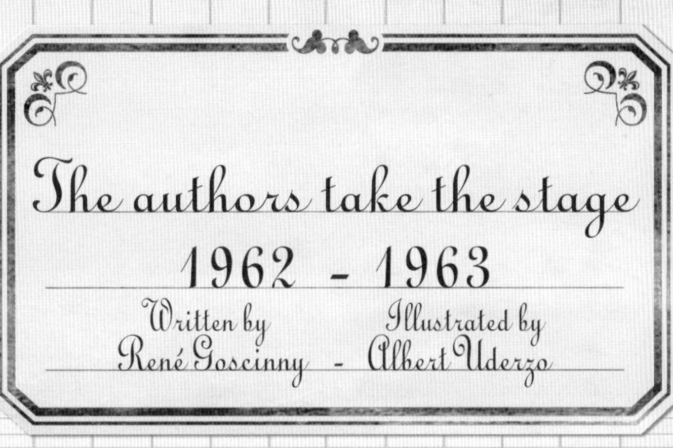

The authors take the stage 1962 - 1963

Written by René Goscinny - Illustrated by Albert Uderzo

Although strip cartoons tend to be written and drawn to a standard pattern today, in the 1960s and 1970s there was more of a libertarian spirit in them, and they often ignored graphic conventions and logical time schemes. Showing the authors in the company of their own creations was almost obligatory — readers expected and wanted it, and indeed that was one of the reasons for the magical sympathy between readers and authors.

It was in this spirit that René and Albert, like many other writers and illustrators of strip cartoons, invented works of pure fantasy in which they crossed the borders of space and time, and finally revealed the true story of the creation of Asterix.

* The power to make people laugh: from an epigram by Caesar on Terence, the Latin poet.

The Obelix family tree
07 February 1963

Written by René Goscinny - Illustrated by Albert Uderzo

(This story was first published in 15 issues of "Pilote", nos 172–186)

I HAVE TO LEAVE ON THE TIDE WITH THAT CONTAINER ABOARD!
IT'S NOT MY FAULT IF THE CRANE BROKE DOWN!

I'LL FIX IT FOR YOU!

WHERE DO I PUT THIS LITTLE PACKAGE?
IN ... IN THE HOLD, PLEASE!
VALPAR
3

DID YOU SEE HIS STRENGTH? DOESN'T IT REMIND YOU OF SOMEONE? I'M JUST WONDERING ...
LET'S NOT LOSE SIGHT OF HIM ... HE'S GOING INTO THAT CAFÉ ...

THE USUAL?
THE USUAL...

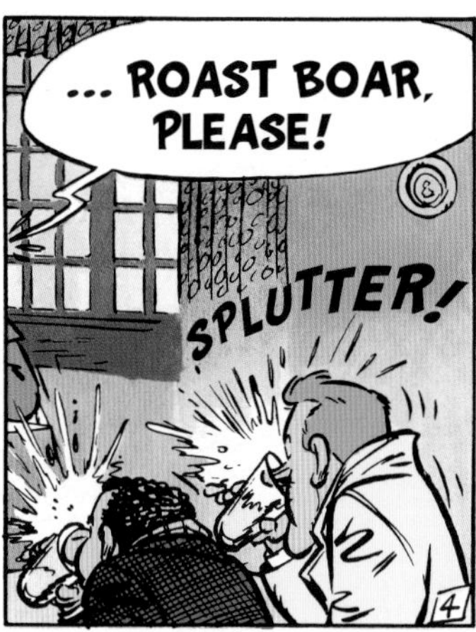
... ROAST BOAR, PLEASE!
SPLUTTER!
4

ER ... EXCUSE US, SIR ... WOULD YOU TELL US YOUR NAME?
WE'RE DOING A LITTLE SURVEY.
?

OF COURSE ... YUM ... GULP! MY NAME'S OBELISC'H ... SCRUNCH ... SAY OBELISK IF YOU LIKE, IT'S EASIER ... YUM ...
THESE PARISIANS ARE CRAZY!

OBELISC'H!
WE ... WE KNOW ONE OF YOUR ANCESTORS VERY WELL. HE'S A FRIEND OF OURS!
THESE PARISIANS ARE TOTALLY CRAZY!
YUM
YUM!
SCRUNCH!
SCRUNCH!
5

I'VE GOT AN OLD DOCUMENT ABOUT MY ANCESTORS AT HOME, IF YOU'RE INTERESTED?
OH YES! YOU BET WE ARE!

6
HERE YOU ARE!
OH, MY WORD!

8
OBELISC'H
7
OBELISC'H
the Fat
FRIEND OF THE PRIVATEER ROBERT SURCOUF, BOTH OF THEM FROM ST MALO. WAS TOLD BY THE EMPEROR NAPOLEON: "I AM PLEASED WITH YOU AND KINDLY DO NOT EAT WHILE I'M TALKING TO YOU!" SCUTTLING THEIR OWN SHIP, HIS ENEMIES SAID: "WE'VE GOT THAT SINKING FEELING AGAIN."
6
OBELISC'H
the Boar
COMPANION OF THE KING'S CORSAIR RENÉ DUGUAY-TROUIN. HIS VANQUISHED ENEMIES DECLARED, "BETTER SCUTTLE OUR OWN SHIP AND THEN SCUTTLE."
5
OBELISC'H
Count of Brittany
FAMOUS FOR WINNING THE FIRST BATTLE OF MARIGNAN (1514) SINGLE-HANDED.
4
OBELISC'H
Lord of the Manor of the Menhir
FOUGHT IN THE 100 YEARS' WAR WITH HIS FRIEND BERTRAND DU GUESCLIN. THE COMMENT, "THESE ENGLISH ARE CRAZY!" IS ATTRIBUTED TO HIM.
LET'S GET THEM! LET'S GET THEM!
FAMILY COAT OF ARMS: A BOAR RECUMBENT ON A BACKGROUND GULES
3
OBELISQUE the Valiant
COVERED HIMSELF WITH GLORY DURING THE CRUSADES. ON HIS RETURN AMAZED HIS FRIENDS BY EATING FOURTEEN BOARS AT A SITTING.
2
OBELISQUE
the Hammer
FLATTENED EVERY ENEMY HE MET. FOUGHT AT POITIERS UNDER CHARLES MARTEL. LED HIS MEN INTO THE ATTACK WITH HIS FAMOUS WARCRY OF: "LET'S GET THEM!" IT WAS IN VAIN THAT HE IMPLORED THE ENEMY NOT TO RUN AWAY.
1
OBELIX
Gaulish warrior
MENHIR DELIVERY MAN, FOUNDER OF THE DYNASTY.

THIS IS GREAT! SO YOU'RE DESCENDED FROM OBELIX THE MENHIR DELIVERY MAN?
ASTERIX'S BEST FRIEND?
THAT'S RIGHT!

YOU MUST COME BACK TO LUTETIA WITH US, OR NO ONE WILL BELIEVE IT!
HE MEANS PARIS.
PARIS?

RIGHT, I'LL JUST GO AND GET MY THINGS!
AND WE'LL GO AND FETCH MY NICE NEW CAR!
THEY'LL BE AMAZED BACK AT THE OFFICE! THEY SAY OUR STORIES ARE ALL MAKE-BELIEVE!
8

IS HE COMING YET?
HERE HE IS!
376-BT5

WHERE CAN I PUT MY BITS AND BOBS?
ON THE LUGGAGE RACK, BUT MIND YOU DON'T SCRATCH THE PAINTWORK OF MY NICE NEW CAR!

BUT YOU SAID PUT IT ON THE ...
9

DO YOU ... DO YOU REALLY HAVE TO BRING THAT MENHIR?
SURE! IN MY FAMILY WE NEVER GO AWAY WITHOUT A MENHIR! IT'S OUR LITTLE LUCKY CHARM!
A BRAND NEW CAR ... HOW AM I GOING TO EXPLAIN THAT TO THE INSURANCE COMPANY?
POC!

A MENHIR HIT THE ROOF, I SAY ... HIT THE ROOF, THEY'LL ASK, OR YOUR HEAD? AND THEY'LL HIT THE ROOF!
HURRY UP! THERE'S A TRAIN COMING!
CUSTOMERS AT LAST! PORTER? PORTER?

WHAT'S UP, HORACE? ANYONE WOULD THINK THE DEVIL WAS AFTER YOU!
LE GOUËT
10

SURE YOU DON'T WANT TO LEAVE YOUR MENHIR IN THE LUGGAGE VAN?
NO FEAR! HISTORICAL RELICS LIKE THIS DON'T TRAVEL IN LUGGAGE VANS!

OH NO YOU DON'T! THAT ... THAT STONE THING TAKES UP AT LEAST TWO SEATS ...
YOU'RE BEGINNING TO GET ME DOWN! I KNOW MY OWN MIND, I DO!

AND TO THINK THAT MENHIR IS TRAVELLING ON A NICE SOFT SEAT!
MAKES SENSE, DOESN'T IT? YOU'RE NOT A HISTORICAL RELIC SO YOU TRAVEL IN THE GUARD'S VAN!
11

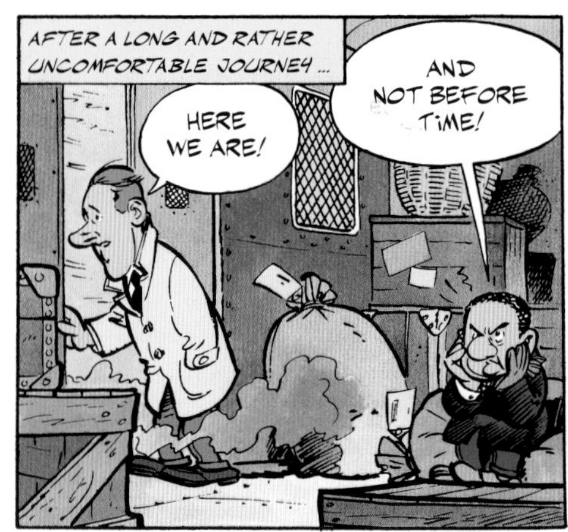
AFTER A LONG AND RATHER UNCOMFORTABLE JOURNEY ...
HERE WE ARE!
AND NOT BEFORE TIME!

HAD A GOOD JOURNEY?
YES, I SLEPT ALL THE WAY. NOW I'M A LITTLE PECKISH.

THE TAXIS WON'T TAKE US, THE UNDERGROUND WON'T LET US ON, THE BUS WON'T HAVE US EITHER!
I DON'T LIKE YOUR ANTI-MENHIRIST PREJUDICES HERE IN PARIS!
CAFÉ
12

HERE WE ARE! THE OFFICES OF OUR MAGAZINE "PILOTE", MY DEAR OBELISC'H. YOU'LL BE A SMASH HIT HERE!
I'LL JUST PUT THE MENHIR DOWN AND TIDY MY HAIR!
Books & Magazines
Pilote
Pilote
Pilote

NOT VERY STRONG, YOUR WINDOWS IN PARIS!
13

HEY, EVERYONE, LOOK WHO'S HERE!!!
EDITOR
Pilote

AND BELIEVE ME, MY DEAR OBELIX ...
OBELISC'H – WITH AN S, A C AND AN H.
ANYONE SEEN MY TYPEWRITER?
POP!
EDITOR
UDERZO
14

AND NOW, MY DEAR OBELISC'H, WE'LL SHOW YOU ROUND THE OFFICES.
THE OFFICES OF "PILOTE"? GREAT!

DOES HE TAKE HIS MENHIR EVERYWHERE?
YES, AND SPEAKING OF THAT ... YOU KNOW MY NEW CAR?
OUUUUCH!

WHO'S THAT GENTLEMAN?
ONLY THE BOSS!
15
THE END

How do they think it all up ? August 1993

"What gave you the idea of Asterix?"

"Who writes the story and who does the drawing?"

"You must have been good at Latin at school, weren't you?"

"Who are you?"

René Goscinny and I were often and regularly asked such questions, and I still have to answer them today, almost forty-five years after our character Asterix was born.

Some of the questions are not quite the same as those we were asked at first. For instance, "Do you actually make a living out of your little so-and-sos?" has become, "Hey, you must earn oodles of boodle with that lot, don't you?" Well, at least that may be a sign that our job has become more respectable.

And we have always appreciated the elegance, delicacy and attention some readers have shown towards us. Even in the 1960s, we liked responding in our own way in "Pilote", the thinking person's strip cartoon magazine, by answering the question of how an idea is born.

Dear readers, on the next page I offer the answer for your mature consideration, asking myself as always the eternal question, "Will they like it?"

Albert Uderzo

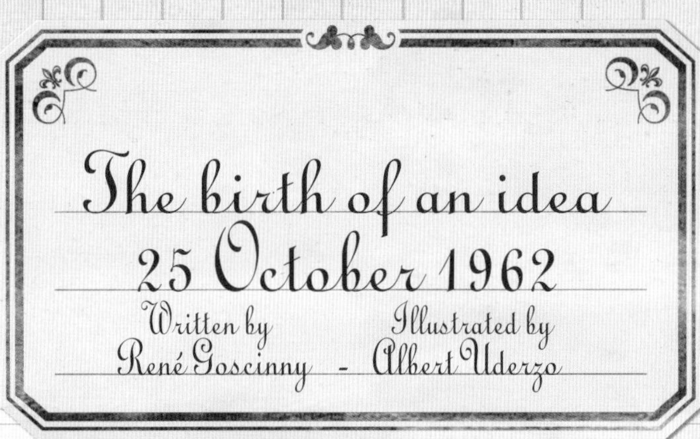
The birth of an idea
25 October 1962
Written by
René Goscinny
Illustrated by
Albert Uderzo

"Pilote", n° 157

ANN
RHUBARBRHUBARB
RHUBARBRHUBARBRHUBARB ...

CRAASH! THEN BOOM! AND TCHAC!
HA, HA, HA!
OH YES! OH YES!

AND THEN ... PATABOOM! CRAAAASH!
PFFFFFFF! TEEHEEHEE! TEEHEEHEE!

BANG! AND THEN ... BING! PAAAF!
TELEPHON
YES, AND THEN WE HAVE ... CRAAACK!

CAFÉ DE L'ANNEXE
FASHIONS
WOOHOOHOO! HO, HO! BOF!
HA HA HA! HO, HO! TEE HEE HEE!
DING! DING! DING!
UDERZO
THE END

R. GOSCINNY Asterix A. UDERZO

Asterix AND THE FALLING SKY

Written and illustrated by Albert UDERZO

-UDERZO-

GOSCINNY AND UDERZO

PRESENT

An Asterix Adventure

ASTERIX AND THE FALLING SKY

Written and Illustrated by ALBERT UDERZO

Translated by Anthea Bell *and* Derek Hockridge

For my brother Bruno, to whom I owe everything.

Bruno (1920-2004) and Albert Uderzo in 1942

Bruno Uderzo was Albert's elder brother. There were seven years between them. It was Bruno who, recognising his younger brother's budding talent, first took him to see a Parisian publisher. That was in the summer of 1940, and Albert was thirteen years old.

Respect, affection and shared interests united the two brothers.

BELGICA
GAULISH VILLAGE
COMPENDIUM
LAUDANUM
AQUARIUM
TOTORUM
LUTETIA
SPQR
ARMORICA
GAUL
(ROMAN CONQUEST)
50 BC
CELTICA
PROVINCIA
AQUITANIA
THE YEAR IS 50 BC. GAUL IS ENTIRELY OCCUPIED BY THE ROMANS. WELL, NOT ENTIRELY ... ONE SMALL VILLAGE OF INDOMITABLE GAULS STILL HOLDS OUT AGAINST THE INVADERS. AND LIFE IS NOT EASY FOR THE ROMAN LEGIONARIES WHO GARRISON THE FORTIFIED CAMPS OF TOTORUM, AQUARIUM, LAUDANUM AND COMPENDIUM ...

SOMETHING TELLS ME THERE'LL BE A GOOD CROP OF BOARS TODAY, ASTERIX!
AS USUAL, OBELIX!

THERE, WHAT DID I SAY?
YES, BUT LOOK! HOW ODD ... THAT ONE'S STIFF AS A BOARD!

WHAT'S HAPPENED TO IT? IT LOOKS BORED RIGID!
?!
?

YUK!
IT'S TOTALLY INEDIBLE!

MUCH LATER ...
THIS ISN'T NORMAL! ALL THE BOARS WE'VE MET SEEM TO HAVE CAUGHT SOME STRANGE DISEASE, ASTERIX!
YOU'RE RIGHT! EVEN THE BIRDS AREN'T SINGING! THIS SILENCE IS VERY STRANGE!
1 A 33

?!
STOP, OBELIX! SOMETHING TELLS ME WE'D BETTER GET BACK TO THE VILLAGE!!!

BUT WHAT ABOUT THE BOARS? WHAT'S TO BECOME OF ME WITHOUT BOARS?
SOME THINGS MATTER MORE THAN THE HEALTH OF OUR BOARS, OBELIX!

WHAT FUNNY IDEAS ASTERIX GETS! IT'S MY HEALTH I'M TALKING ABOUT!

AND NOW I'M HUNGRY, SO THERE!
GRRRRR!!!
1 B 33
-UDERZO-

HI THERE, FULLIAUTOMATIX! HAVE YOU NOTICED ANYTHING SPECIAL IN THE ...???

HEY! YOU! CAN YOU HEAR ME?

HE ... HE'S GONE RIGID TOO!!!

FISHMONGER
UNHYGIENIC
FISHMONG
?!?
?!

THIS IS CRAZY! THEY HAVE THE SAME SYMPTOMS AS THE BOARS! QUICK! I MUST GO AND WARN CHIEF VITALSTATISTIX!
2A
33

OH NO! POOR IMPEDIMENTA! IS SHE INFECTED TOO? LET'S JUST HOPE THAT ...

'SCUSE ME, IMPEDIMENTA, BUT THIS IS URGENT!

CHIEF! CHIEF! CHIEF?!?

BY TOUTATIS!!! THE WHOLE VILLAGE IS IN THE GRIP OF THIS PECULIAR PHENOMENON!!!

THIS IS A NIGHTMARE, OBELIX!
OH, SO NOW YOU ADMIT IT'S NO JOKE!!!
?
2B
33

-UDERZO-

QUICK, LET'S GO AND SEE OUR DRUID! PERHAPS HE'S ESCAPED THIS DISASTER!

YES! PRAISE BE TO TOUTATIS! I CAN SEE HIM MOVING!

IT'S INCREDIBLE, ALL THE ANIMALS IN THE FOREST AND ALL THE VILLAGERS SEEM TO HAVE CAUGHT SOME STRANGE DISEASE WHICH LEAVES THEM PARALYSED!!! HOW ON EARTH DID YOU ESCAPE?
I'VE NO IDEA WHAT YOU'RE TALKING ABOUT, ASTERIX!!

ALL I KNOW IS THAT I'D FINISHED MAKING A CAULDRON OF MAGIC POTION! I'D JUST BEEN TASTING IT WHEN I NOTICED A STRANGE NUMB FEELING COMING OVER ME!!!
?!
SNIFF! SNIFF!
3A 33

UNLESS I'M MUCH MISTAKEN, WE ALONE HAVE BEEN SPARED BY THIS STRANGE PHENOMENON! HOW DO WE EXPLAIN THAT, ASTERIX?
I THINK I KNOW THE ANSWER!

SO WHAT IS IT?
ELEMENTARY! THE MAGIC POTION!

VERY LUCKILY, YOU TASTED ENOUGH OF YOUR POTION TO WARD OFF THE EFFECTS OF THIS DISEASE! I DRANK SOME MYSELF BEFORE I WENT BOAR-HUNTING ...

AND WITH OBELIX THE QUESTION DOESN'T ARISE!
ENORMOUS SIGH!

ALTHOUGH IT COULD HAVE ARISEN WITH DOGMATIX, AND LIKE US HE'S HAD NO PROBLEMS!

OBELIX! COME ON, CONFESS! YOU'VE BEEN FEEDING DOGMATIX POTION!
ONLY A FEW TINY LITTLE DROPS ... NOTHING AT ALL TO SPEAK OF!
WOOF!
WOOF!
3B 33

- UDERZO -

WELL DONE, ASTERIX! I SEE THAT YOU AT LEAST RETAIN YOUR COMMON SENSE!
YES, BUT ...

... WE'RE COUNTING ON YOU, O DRUID, TO FIND A MAGIC FORMULA THAT WILL HELP OUR FRIENDS TO SNAP OUT OF THEIR PARALYSIS!!!
AND THE BOARS TOO!
?!!

AS I DON'T KNOW THE CAUSE OF THE PHENOMENON AFFLICTING OUR VILLAGE ...

... I DON'T SEE HOW I CAN FIND A CURE, ASTERIX!
OH, COME ON! WE KNOW THE POTION IMMUNISES US!
DO YOU THINK WE COULD GIVE SOME TO THE BOARS, AST ...
4A 33

OBELIX! YOU AND YOUR BOARS ARE SERIOUSLY BEGINNING TO GET ME DOWN! I'VE ALREADY TOLD YOU WE HAVE MORE IMPORTANT PRIORITIES THAN THOSE BOARS!!!
?
SO THERE IT IS! SOON I'LL BE A MERE SHADOW OF MYSELF!
GRRR!
WOOF!
WOOF!

?!?
YELP!
4B 33
- UDERZO -

BY TOUTATIS!!!
WHAT ON EARTH IS THIS HORRIBLE THING COMING DOWN TO CRUSH US?
5 33

?!
?!
?!

OH, 'SCUSE ME! I FORGOT TO TRANSLATE INTO YOUR LANGUAGE WITH MY COMTUPER ... SORRY, MY COMPUTER!

WHO ARE YOU, AND WHERE DO YOU COME FROM?
AND WHAT'S THAT ENORMOUS THINGY YOU GOT OUT OF?
LET ME EXPLAIN!
6A 33

I HAVE COME FROM THE DISTANT STAR TADSILWENY IN MY INTERSTELLAR SPACECRAFT UP THERE! DO I INTRUDE?

WHATEVER DOES HE MEAN?
I THINK THIS SHRINKING VIOLET IS TELLING US HE CAME FROM A STAR IN THAT HUGE CHARIOT, BUT IN TERMS I DON'T REALLY UNDERSTAND!

I CAN SEE THAT YOUR CIVILISATION IS MUCH MORE PRIMITIVE THAN OURS!
SNIFF! SNIFF!

ARE YOU TRYING TO TAKE THE MICKEY, YOU NOT-SO-SHRINKING VIOLET? IF SO, YOU CAN JUST GET BACK INTO YOUR TADDYTHINGY AND PUSH OFF!!!
?
KEEP CALM! LET'S TRY TO UNDERSTAND!
ZAP!

TCHOK!
!?
6B 33
UDERZO

SO JUST WHAT'S THAT?
A CLONE. A SUPERCLONE WHO MISCALCULATED YOUR TERRESTRIAL FORCE OF GRAVITY. IT'S MUCH STRONGER THAN OURS AT HOME!

SUPERCLONES ARE OUR SECURITY MEN. THEY KEEP THE PEACE!
SNIFF! SNIFF!

AND WHEN THEIR SUMS WORK OUT RIGHT, THEY CAN MOVE AROUND EASILY THANKS TO ANTI-GRAVITY!
?!

DO YOU UNDERSTAND ANY OF THIS, GETAFIX?
NO, ASTERIX! I DON'T KNOW IF IT'S A DREAM OR A NIGHTMARE!

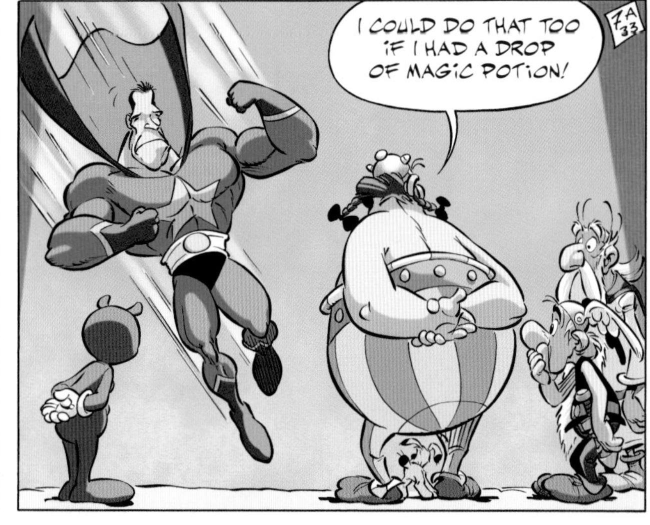
7A 33
I COULD DO THAT TOO IF I HAD A DROP OF MAGIC POTION!

WHAT'S HE SAYING?

HE ONLY SAID "FAT CHANCE!"
WHAT WAS THAT?

- UDERZO - 7B 33

DZING!
BONG!
TCHAC!
I ... AM ... NOT FAT!

REALLY! I ASK YOU!

WOULDN'T YOU SAY OBELIX HAS THE ANTI-GRAVITY KNACK TOO?
PLEASE FORGIVE OUR FRIEND. HE'S VERY SENSITIVE ON SOME SUBJECTS!
NEVER MIND! THE CLONE WILL GET OVER IT!
AND WE CAN ALWAYS RE-CLONE HIM IF NECESSARY, AS EITHER A SPIDER OR A BAT SUPERCLONE!
?!?
8A 33

HE NEVER BEARS A GRUDGE EITHER, SO YOUR FRIEND CAN ASK HIM ANY LITTLE FAVOUR HE LIKES!
!

RIGHT! LET'S FORGET ALL THAT ... ER ... YOU ABLE DO ME LITTLE FAVOUR?
YOU CAN TALK NORMALLY. HIS COMPUTER WILL RE-TRANSMIT IT IN HIS OWN LANGUAGE!

YOU BRING ME THAT?

THAT BE WILD BOAR! YOU COMPRENNY?

WE'LL SEE IF THAT SOFTY IS AS GOOD AS ME AT CATCHING BOARS!
OBELIX, YOU'RE HOPELESS!
8B 33

-UDERZO-

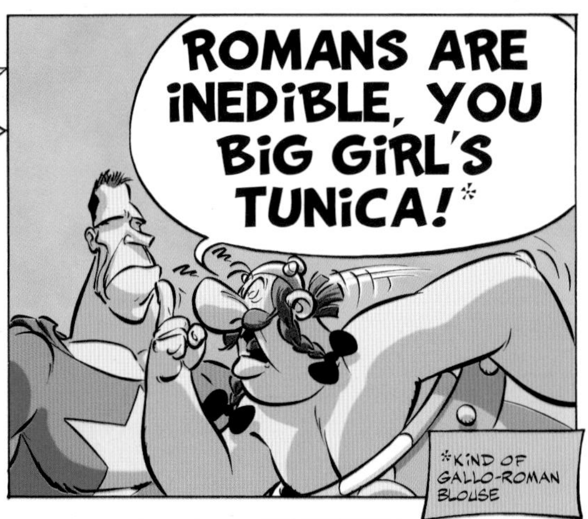

*KIND OF GALLO-ROMAN BLOUSE

- UDERZO -

PHEW! AT LAST, BOYS! THAT MONSTER IS MOVING AWAY. WE CAN SEE THE SUN AGAIN!

COCK-A-DOODLE-DO!

AND THE VILLAGE IS COMING BACK TO LIFE, GETAFIX!!!

10A 33

-UDERZO-05

PIF!
PAF!
BING!
HOW DARE YOU START A PUNCH-UP WITHOUT ME, YOU YOUNG RASCALS!

BY BELENOS, HOW NICE TO SEE OUR VILLAGE BACK TO NORMAL!!!

WHERE ARE YOU GOING, OBELIX?
INTO THE FOREST TO SEE IF THE BOARS HAVE COME BACK TO LIFE!
FISHMONGER UNHYGIENIX FISHMONGER

WELL, YOU ROMANS HAVE A NERVE AND NO MISTAKE!!
ER ... IT'S LIKE THIS, MA'AM ... YOU'LL LAUGH, BUT ...
... WE HAVE NO IDEA AT ALL HOW WE GOT INTO YOUR VILLAGE!!
OH NO?
11A 33

POC!
TCHAC!
BING!

WELL, NOW YOU KNOW HOW YOU'RE GETTING OUT OF IT AGAIN!

PAF!

WE LIVE IN INTERESTING TIMES, ASTERIX!
DO WE? I WISH THEY'D JUST GET BACK TO THAT CIVILISED STAR OF THEIRS!

I THINK IT'S TIME I TOLD YOU WHY WE'RE HERE!
FOILED AGAIN!

HE CERTAINLY NEEDS SOME REPAIR WORK!!
TCHOF!
11B 33

-UDERZO-

I DIDN'T KNOW THERE WAS GOING TO BE A FANCY-DRESS PARTY AROUND HERE!
OR MAYBE THE ROMAN LEGIONARIES HAVE NEW UNIFORMS?

HOW ODD – YOU LOT ALL LOOK DIFFERENT! BACK HOME IN TADSILWENY WE'RE ALL IDENTICAL! THAT MAKES IT EASIER FOR US TO RECOGNISE EACH OTHER!
!?!

OOH, LOOK AT THE BIG MAN'S BEAUTIFUL BICEPS!
I'LL GIVE YOU BEAUTIFUL BICEPS! SCRAM! GET AWAY HOME!

AND JUST WHO ARE THESE ODDBALLS?
12A
33

?!?
BEINGS FROM ANOTHER WORLD WHO HAVE COME ALL THE WAY HERE IN THEIR ODD METAL BALL!
!?
!

THE SKY IS ABOUT TO FALL ON OUR HEADS!
12B
33

-UDERZO-

I WISH I KNEW WHAT THIS IS ALL ABOUT! TAKE THOSE TWO WEIRDOS TO MY HUT!

A LITTLE LATER ...
SO YOU'RE ALL SPACED OUT, ARE YOU? YOU MUST BE OVER THE MOON TO HAVE COME DOWN TO EARTH!
WE ARE FROM A GALAXY OF FIFTY STARS, ALL OF THEM AT PEACE WITH THEIR NEIGHBOURS!

OH, SO IT'S YOU WE SEE ALL LIT UP ABOVE OUR HEADS AT NIGHT!
NO, OUR STARS BURNED OUT LONG AGO, AND WE TRAVEL FASTER THAN THE SPEED OF LIGHT!
?
?

THAT'S ENOUGH LIGHT CONVERSATION. WHAT ARE YOU DOING HERE?
THE GALACTIC COUNCIL OF THE WISE HAS SENT ME TO WARN YOU OF A REAL AND PRESENT DANGER ... THE NAGMAS!

YOU JUST LISTEN TO ME! WE FEAR ONLY ONE THING: THE SKY FALLING ON OUR HEADS!
HERE WE GO AGAIN!
13A 33

THAT'S THE POINT! THE UNSCRUPULOUS NAGMAS KNOW THAT YOU HAVE A SECRET WEAPON, AND THEY'RE GOING TO FALL ON YOU TO GET HOLD OF IT.
BUT HOW DO YOU KNOW WE HAVE A SECRET WEAPON?
AND WHAT ARE YOU GOING TO DO TO STOP THEM?

THE WHOLE UNIVERSE KNOWS ABOUT YOUR WEAPON, AND FOR SAFETY'S SAKE MY MISSION IS TO CONFISCATE IT!
!?!

I WAS HIS SIZE MYSELF WHEN I WAS YOUNGER!
YOUR HEAD WAS HIS SIZE, YES! THEY CALLED YOU SAFETY-PINHEAD AS A CHILD!
PFFFF!!

YOU THINK THAT'S FUNNY, DO YOU?
SO WHAT IF I DO?
13B 33

- UDERZO -

*LATIN CELL

-UDERZO-

I'LL GIVE THEM WEIRDOS FLYING OUT OF SOME GREAT BIG ...
WWWOOO!

JUST WHAT DOES SOME JOKER THINK HE'S UP TO NOW?
WWOOOUUU

?!!
WOOOT!HA

TCHHOOOO
CREAK!
CREAK!

GASP! GET TO SHELTER! GASP! PANT!
GET YOUR WEAPONS! PANT! GASP!
GET HELP! PANT! GASP!
PFFFFCHCH
15A 33

BY JUPITER, WHAT'S THAT MONSTER?
WE TOLD YOU THERE WAS SOMETHING FUNNY IN THE AIR JUST NOW, CENTURION!
15B 33

UDERZO

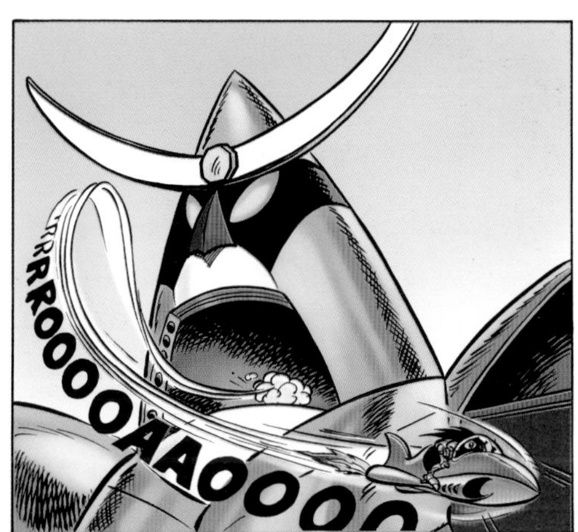

THEN YOU IS HAVING VERY POWERFUL DEADLY WEAPON?

OH, YOU MEAN THE MAGIC POTION, MY DEAR SIR! NO, WE DON'T HAVE THE POTION, WE JUST FEEL ITS AFTER-EFFECTS, BUT YOU'LL FIND IT IN THE GAULISH VILLAGE ON THE OTHER SIDE OF THE FOREST! YOU CAN'T MISS IT ... THEY HAVE A BIG FAT MAN THERE WHO'S PERMANENTLY STUFFED WITH POTION!

-UDERZO-

MEANWHILE, IN THE GAULISH VILLAGE ...
BUT WHO ARE THESE NAGMAS WHO SCARE YOU SO MUCH?
THEY COME FROM THE PLANET GMANA AND WANT TO BE SOLE MASTERS OF THE UNIVERSE!

HUH! LET THEM COME! WE'LL SOON DEAL WITH THEM. WELCOME TO OUR VILLAGE, ER ... WHAT'S YOUR NAME?
MY NAME IS TOON.

I'M ASTERIX, AND THIS IS OUR DRUID GETAFIX, THE WISEST AND CLEVEREST MAN IN THE VILLAGE!
OUR GREAT SAGE AT HOME IN TADSILWENY IS CALLED HUBS!

OH, I THOUGHT YOU HAD HICCUPS! MY DEAR TOON, WE'D BE DELIGHTED TO ASK YOU TO DINNER, BUT WE'RE SHORT OF BOARS AT THE MOMENT!
THEN LET ME INVITE YOU TO TASTE OUR FAVOURITE FOOD!
SNAP

IT'S A HOT DOG. DELICIOUS, AND GIVES YOU LOTS OF ENERGY!
!?

YUK! NO THANKS, REALLY!
17A 33

YOU KNOW, DOGMATIX, I'M REALLY GLAD TO KNOW THE BOARS ARE IN GOOD HEALTH AGAIN ...
WOOF!

?

WRRAAOOOOOOUMM!
HELP!
THIS TIME THE ROMANS HAVE GONE TOO FAR!!!
17B 33
UDERZO

WHAT SORT
OF WEIRDO
IS THIS?

IF YOU HAVE BIG
HEAP DEADLY WEAPONS,
YOU HAND THEM OVER!
IF HE THINKS HE'S
GETTING MY BOARS HE'S
GOT A PUNCH-UP
COMING!

AND IF YOU RESIST
FIRE OF HEAVEN, YOU
DO HAVE DEADLY
WEAPON!
TZZIOOO..
18A
33

OH GREAT
SAGE AKOAOTAKI,
ME FOUND DEADLY
WEAPON!
AND I'VE LOST
MY TWO BOARS,
I HAVE!

NOW YOU GIVE ME
SECRET DEADLY
WEAPON OR
ELSE ...
AND YOU GIVE ME BACK MY BOARS,
YOU STUPID GREAT GRASSHOPPER,
OR ELSE ...

YEEEE!
TCHOC!
18B
33

-UDERZO-

SPLONTCH

TCHAC
POTCH!
ZMMNN

PATCHOC
ZONG

?

BLING BLANG
I CAN MAKE PLENTY OF NOISE TOO!
BLONG BLUNG

COME ON, DOGMATIX. LET'S GET OUT OF HERE BEFORE I LOSE MY TEMPER!
POC!

WHERE ARE YOU, DOGMATIX? I CAN'T SEE YOU, AND THIS NOISE IS DEAFENING!
WOOF! WOOF!
POC!

OH NO! I'VE LOST MY BOARS AND DOGMATIX TOO!!!
?!

IN ASTERIX'S HUT ...
HOW EXACTLY ARE YOU AND THE NAGMAS DIFFERENT?
THE NAGMAS ARE ENVIOUS AND VINDICTIVE! THEY COPY US, BUT THEIR SCIENTIFIC KNOWLEDGE LAGS BEHIND OURS!

SO THEY NEED TO GET HOLD OF SECRET WEAPONS DEVELOPED BY PRIMITIVE PEOPLE LIKE US!

ASTERIX! GETAFIX!
?
?

LOOK WHAT SOME WEIRDO WENT AND DID TO DOGMATIX!
THAT'S THE WORK OF A NAGMA!

DOGMATIX? BUT WHERE IS HE?
HERE, BUT HE'S IN POOR SHAPE!
20A 33

I NEARLY STOOD ON HIM AND CRUSHED HIM! DO SOMETHING, GETAFIX!
I'M AFRAID THERE'S NOTHING I CAN DO, MY DEAR OBELIX!
JUDGING BY THE RESULTS, THE POTION HAD WORN OFF HIM.
WOOF! WOOF!

MOVE ASIDE. I MAY BE ABLE TO DO SOMETHING!
!

HE'S BACK IN GOOD SHAPE! THANKS, SHRINKING VIOLET!
WOOF!
PCHOT

LUCKILY WE CAN COUNTER ALL THEIR WEAPONS – JUST AS THEY CAN COUNTER OURS. THAT'S THE PROBLEM!!
?
!

JUST BETWEEN US, COULD YOU BRING MY BOARS BACK?

WATCH OUT!! A STRANGE FLYING OBJECT IS MAKING FOR THE VILLAGE!!!
20B 33

-UDERZO-

NAOUU
? ? ? ? ? ? ? ? ?

WAAHOOOOOOOO
IT'S GOING TO SET THE VILLAGE ALIGHT!
I'LL GO BACK UP TO MY STARSHIP, ASTERIX!

BRAC OOFF
JUMP, CACOFONIX!
21A 33

TCHOC!

THIS TIME HE REALLY HAS BROUGHT THE HOUSE DOWN!
GASP, GASP!

?!
BOING!
21B 33

UDERZO

WELL DONE, AND THANK YOU! BUT FOR YOU OUR VILLAGE WOULD BE GOING UP IN SMOKE!!
I TOLD YOU, NAGMAS ARE DANGEROUS!

RRROHAOUUU
THERE'S THE ONE WHO STOLE MY BOARS! WATCH OUT, ASTERIX! HE'LL STEAL SOMETHING FROM YOU TOO!
?
?!

ME WANT MAKE PEACE WITH LITTLE EARTHMEN!
YOU DO?
HE DOESN'T TALK LIKE US EITHER! HE TALKS FUNNY!

ME MAKE BETTER OFFER THAN TADSILWENYAN! ME EXCHANGE NAGMA WEAPON FOR DEADLY EARTH WEAPON!
GLUG! GLUG!
LET'S MOVE OFF. WHEN ASTERIX DRINKS THAT TOAST SOMEONE GETS A GRILLING!
22A 33

SWING!

SPLING!

NOT A BAD EXCHANGE!

BZZZZZZ!

PEUTPEUTPEUTPEUTPEUTPEUT
?!
THE CYBERATS!
22B 33
-UDERZO-

PEUTPEUTPEUTPEUTPEUTPEUT

23B
33

UDERZO

WHY IS THIS ROGER OUT? DID TOON BOWL HIM OVER? THAT'S NOT CRICKET ...
WITH THE MEANS THEY SEEM TO HAVE AT THEIR DISPOSAL, THIS COULD GET STICKY ...
I HOPE THE TADSILWENYAN WINS!
OOH, LOOK AT THOSE BIG MUSCLE-MEN! I HOPE THEY WIN!
YEAH? YOU GO TO MY HUT AND SEE IF I'M THERE, MISSUS!
24 A 33

WAAOOOOOOOOO
WOOOOAARRR
24 B 33

WAOOOOOOOOOOO
ZWAOOOOOUUUUU
PHEW! ALL THAT NOISE FOR NOTHING! JUST HOT AIR! LET'S GO FOR A WALK, DOGMATIX!
24 C 33
UDERZO

?

THAT'S FUNNY ... THEY'VE ALREADY STOPPED FIGHTING!

BATTLE NO USE! EVENLY MATCHED! WE NEED FIND SOLUTION!
YOU'RE RIGHT, NAGMA! HOW DO YOU SUGGEST WE RESTORE PEACE?

LOOK, GETAFIX, THEY SEEM TO HAVE COME TO SOME AGREEMENT. I DON'T LIKE THIS AT ALL! WE MUST WATCH OUT!
YOU'RE RIGHT, ASTERIX! I'LL GO AND MAKE A QUICK CAULDRON OF MAGIC POTION. YOU NEVER KNOW!
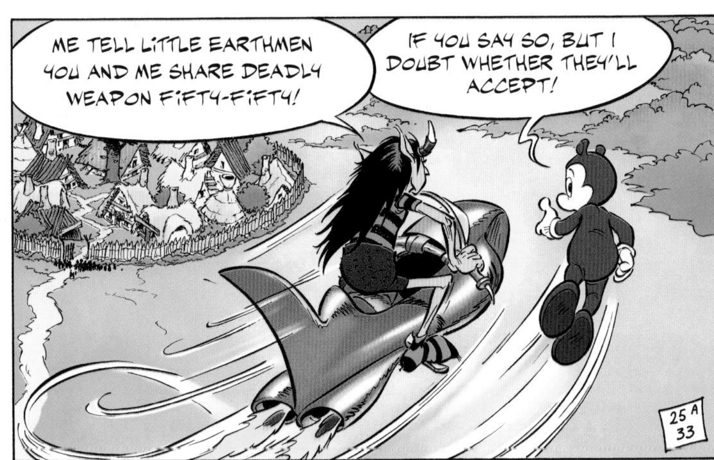
ME TELL LITTLE EARTHMEN YOU AND ME SHARE DEADLY WEAPON FIFTY-FIFTY!
IF YOU SAY SO, BUT I DOUBT WHETHER THEY'LL ACCEPT!
25 A
33

O CHIEF, WE MUST PREPARE FOR THE WORST!
I'VE JUST HAD IT! THOSE TWO FOOLS LET ME DOWN AGAIN!

ME MAKE PEACE WITH TADSILWENYAN...
... BUT IT'S YOU WHO CAN HELP US DO THE DEAL.
I'VE AN IDEA YOU'RE ABOUT TO START ON ABOUT THE SECRET WEAPON AGAIN!

THAT RIGHT! YOU GIVE SECRET WEAPON, WE SHARE FIFTY-FIFTY, WE GO BACK TO STARS!
HMMNNGNNN!

ONLY OUR DRUID KNOWS THE SECRET OF THE MAGIC POTION, SO GET OUT OF HERE AND LEAVE US IN PEACE!!!
?
25B
33
- UDERZO -

WELL, LET'S GO AND SEE THIS DRUID WHO LOOKS SO WISE!
OH NO! IF ONLY THE CHIEF HAD KEPT HIS MOUTH SHUT!

NO! NO! DON'T YOU MOVE FROM HERE! I'LL GO AND FIND HIM.
?!
!
!

NOW THEY KNOW THAT GETAFIX HAS THE SECRET OF THE WEAPON THEY'RE AFTER, OUR DRUID IS IN DANGER!

... THEY'LL WANT TO TASTE YOUR MAGIC POTION, GETAFIX! YOU MUST GET OUT OF HERE AND TAKE SHELTER!!!
OH, IF THAT'S THE PRICE WE MUST PAY FOR PEACE, LET'S GIVE THEM WHAT THEY CAME FOR, ASTERIX!
26A
33

SOON AFTERWARDS ...
EACH OF THEM WILL GET A JAR OF POTION TO TAKE BACK TO THEIR STARS!
I DON'T TRUST THAT NAGMA ONE BIT!

HERE'S THE WEAPON YOU CAME FOR. WE CALL IT "MAGIC POTION"!
?!

BUT ... BUT HOW DOES IT WORK?
EASY. I'LL SHOW YOU. YOU JUST HAVE TO DRINK A MOUTHFUL AND YOU HAVE SUPERHUMAN STRENGTH!

NO, NO! ME NOT DRINK! IT POISON TO TRAP US!
I THOUGHT AS MUCH! HERE, ASTERIX! YOU'LL JUST HAVE TO SACRIFICE YOURSELF!
SIGH!

OH, OBELIX, YOU'VE COME JUST AT THE RIGHT TIME, YOU AND YOUR MENHIR!
YIPPEE! DO I GET SOME MAGIC POTION TOO?
?!
GLUG! GLUG!
26B
33

-UDERZO-

MOVE BACK A BIT, OBELIX! I WANT YOU TO THROW YOUR MENHIR AT ASTERIX, AND HE'LL CATCH IT!
RIGHT! I WAS JUST WONDERING ...
UTOMATIX
?
?

READY, OBELIX! CHUCK IT OVER!
MY WORD! HAVE OUR DRUID AND ASTERIX GONE BACK TO CHILDHOOD?!
FUL

!?!
...
PAF!

THIS IS OUR NATIONAL GAME. WE CALL IT MENHIR-BALL!
YOUR TURN! CATCH!
I REALLY DON'T SEE WHAT'S SO FUNNY ABOUT THIS!
27A 33

ME DRINK MAGIC POTION FIRST!
DON'T PUSH! THERE'LL BE PLENTY FOR EVERYONE!

GLUG! GLUG! GLUG!

YOU WAIT ... AFTER DRINKING THIS, YOU'LL BE ABLE TO MOVE MOUNTAINS!

OBELIX! THE NAGMA IS READY! YOU CAN THROW HIM YOUR MENHIR!
I CAN? RIGHT!
GLUG! GLUG! GLUG!

!
?
TCHONG!
!
27B 33

- UDERZO -

I SHOULD HAVE GUESSED IT WAS THE WRONG POTION, O DRUID!
BUT IT WASN'T! IT WAS THE RIGHT ONE, ASTERIX! YOU DRANK SOME YOURSELF!
?

LOOKS LIKE I HAD A LUCKY ESCAPE!
I CAN'T THINK OF ANY EXPLANATION, UNLESS YOUR CONSTITUTION IS DIFFERENT FROM OURS.
THIS ONE SEEMS A PRETTY HARD NUT TO CRACK!

I DON'T THINK I WANT TO KNOW WHAT HE'S SAYING!

WATCH OUT! HE'S SURE TO WANT HIS REVENGE!
28A
33

PEUTPEUTPEUTPEUTPEUT
I THOUGHT AS MUCH! HE'S SETTING HIS CYBERATS ON YOU.

I'LL GO BACK TO MY SPACESHIP FOR REINFORCEMENTS!
OH, OBELIX AND I CAN COPE WITH THIS! JUST LEND US A COUPLE OF YOUR SUPERCLONES, WOULD YOU?

ALL RIGHT, BUT TAKE MY ADVICE! NEVER ATTACK CYBERATS HEAD ON. THEY HAVE VERY POWERFUL COSMIC WEAPONS.
DON'T WORRY! I HAVE A CUNNING PLAN!

SO HAVE YOU GOT THE IDEA, OBELIX!
OOH, YES! GOODY, GOODY! WE'RE GOING TO HAVE FUN, ASTERIX!

RIGHT, YOU SUPERCLONES! WHEN I SAY **NOW** YOU SEPARATE!
THIS WOULD BE A GREAT WAY TO DELIVER MENHIRS!
28B
33

-UDERZO-

TCHRAC!

IT'S MUCH MORE FUN LIKE THIS!

GOOD SHOT, OBELIX! **OCULUS TAURI!***

29B 33

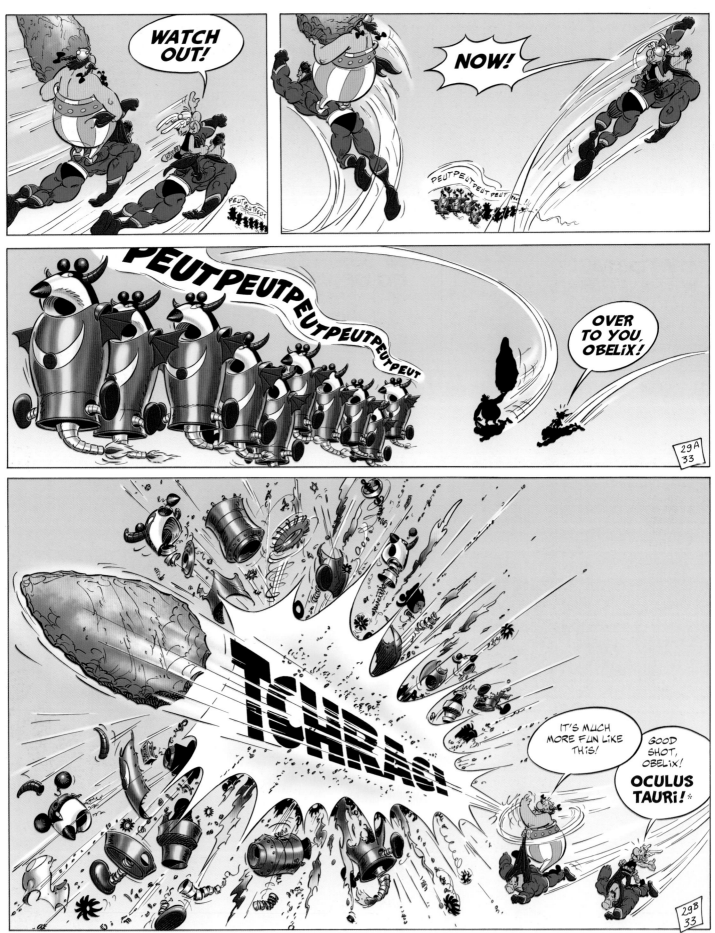

* BULL'S-EYE IN GALLO-ROMAN TIMES.

SOON AFTERWARDS ...
YOUR SUPERCLONES DO A GOOD JOB, MY DEAR TOON!
CAN I SWAP YOU ONE FOR A MENHIR?
OH, REALLY, OBELIX!

NOOOOO!
?!
WHAT'S WRONG? WHAT DID I SAY?
WAAOUUU

BY TOUTATIS, WE MUST SAVE OUR DRUID GETAFIX!
I'LL GO BACK TO MY SPACESHIP AGAIN, ASTERIX!
?!

YOU JUST LET GO OF ME, YOU NASTY WOODLOUSE, YOU!
OLD SORCERER TRICK ME! HIM COME TO STAR NAGMA, MAKE REAL SECRET WEAPON!
30A 33

YOU SAY GOODBYE TO PLANET EARTH, SORCERER!
WRROAOO

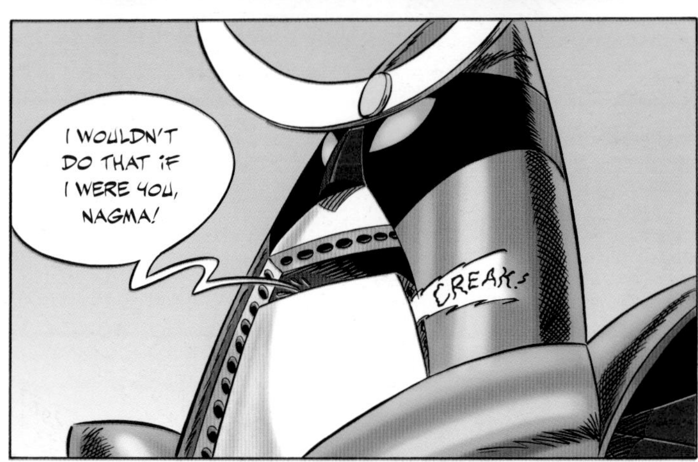
I WOULDN'T DO THAT IF I WERE YOU, NAGMA!
CREAK

WRAOOOAA
30B 33

-UDERZO-

WA
OA

BONG!
?
PRO
AAOO
31A
33

!!?
ROOF
AA

CREAK
RROOO
POUF!
POUF!
POUF!
CRAAAC
31B
33

- UDERZO -

TOON HAS STOPPED THE EViL NAGMA'S ROCKET iN iTS TRACKS!

BUT HOW ARE WE GOiNG TO FREE GETAFiX FROM THiS MONSTROUS MACHiNE?
I CLiMBED THE SPHiNX ONCE, REMEMBER, ASTERiX?* I CAN CLiMB THiS HEAP OF OLD iRON TOO!
* SEE ASTERIX AND CLEOPATRA

LET YOUR PRISONER GO AND I'LL RELEASE YOUR SPACESHIP, NAGMA!

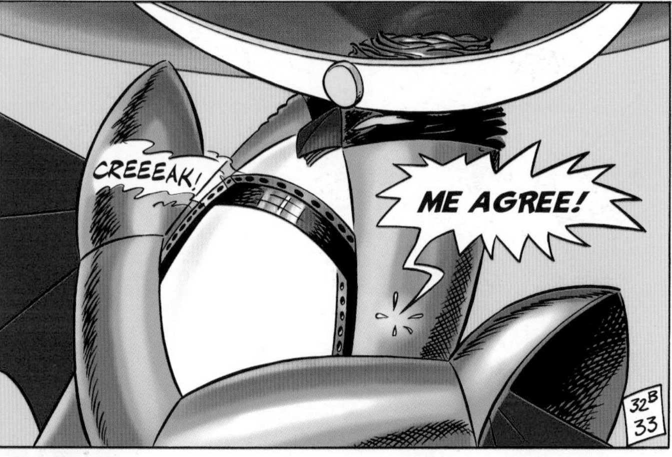
CREEEAK!
ME AGREE!

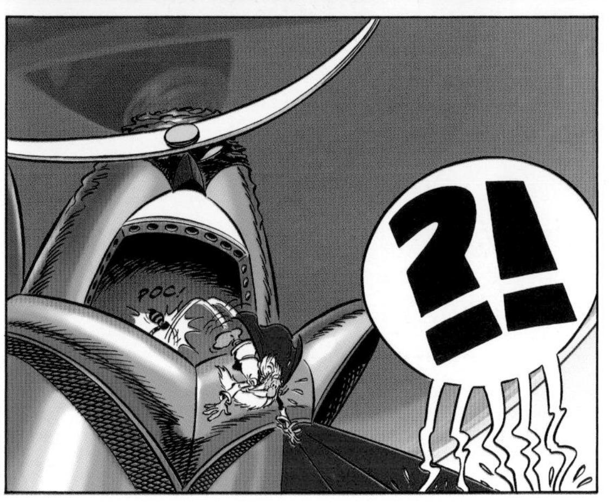
POC!
?!

BY BELENOS!!! OUR DRUiD WiLL FALL AND BE CRUSHED!

NEXT TiME I'LL TRY COOKiNG UP A POTiON TO MAKE ME FLY LiKE OUR TADSiLWENYAN FRiEND!

- UDERZO -

* IN HOMAGE TO THE GREAT GALLO-ROMAN ACTORS LAURUS AND HARDIUS

WWWRRROOOAAAA
?!
SPCHHH!

GIDDY GOAT'S HORNS! THESE NEW GAULISH WEAPONS OUGHT TO BE BANNED BY THE GENAVA CONVENTION!*
NIHIL CONVENIENS DECRETIS EIUS!
THE PILOT OUGHT TO BE FIRED!
*GENEVA

BUT AFTER ITS REFRESHING FOOTBATH, THE ROCKET, NO LONGER A DAMP SQUIB, IS BACK ON COURSE.
ME NEVER COME BACK TO EARTH AGAIN!
34A 33

MEANWHILE, IN THE ROMAN CAMP OF COMPENDIUM ...
LOOK! THAT MONSTER'S MACHINE IS LEAVING THE GAULISH VILLAGE!
WE MUST GO AND TELL CENTURION POLYANTHUS!

IF WHAT YOU SAY IS TRUE, THE GAULS' VILLAGE MUST HAVE BEEN FLATTENED, JUST LIKE OUR CAMP! HO! HO! HO! OUR TURN FOR A GO AT THEM NOW!

AND I PROMOTE YOU TO OPTIONES.* NOW GIVE THE SIGNAL FOR EVERYONE TO FALL IN!
*A KIND OF NCO

LEGIONARIES, THE VILLAGE OF THOSE CRAZY INVINCIBLE GAULS HAS BEEN RAZED TO THE GROUND! WE WILL NOW OCCUPY IT FOR THE GREATER GLORY OF ROME!

ARE YOU WITH ME!
YESSIR!
34B 33
UDERZO

AND THIS TIME, FOR A CHANGE, THE TABLE IS LAID FOR THE BANQUET UNDER THE SUNNY SKIES OF ARMORICA ...

LADIES AND GENTLEMEN, NOBLE GAULS! IT IS WITH DEEP EMOTION THAT I NOW CONVEY, IN MY OWN NAME AND ON BEHALF OF THE WHOLE VILLAGE, THE GREAT JOY WE FEEL IN RETURNING, THANKS TO OUR FRIENDS FROM ANOTHER WORLD, TO A STATE OF TRANQUILLITY AND PEACE, AND ...

WHY AREN'T OUR FRIENDS THE SUPERCLONES HERE TOO?

THEY ONLY EAT HOT DOGS!

THEY EAT **WHAT?**

WHERE'S THE BARD?

CALM DOWN, GERIATRIX, DO!

DON'T WORRY, THERE'S NO DANGER! HE'S GONE INTO THE FOREST TO PRACTISE ON HIS NEW HARP IN PEACEFUL NATURAL SURROUNDINGS!

GRRR!

35B 33

UDERZO

CAN YOU WARN THE SUPERCLONES AND GET THEM TO MOVE YOUR SPHERE AWAY SO AS NOT TO SCARE THE ROMANS?

-UDERZO-

THAT'S A FUNNY THING, CENTURION! UNLIKE OUR CAMP, THEIR VILLAGE SEEMS TO BE INTACT!
COME, COME, OPTIO! CAN'T YOU SEE IT'S ON FIRE?

?
ATTACK THEM!
BANG!
37A 33

PFFRRRAAARG!

WELL, TOON, WHAT DO YOU THINK OF THAT?
AMAZING! WHAT A PITY YOUR MAGIC POTION WOULDN'T DO US ANY GOOD!
WHEN THE GAULS HAVE GONE, BRING ME THOSE TWO TWITS WHO GAVE ME THIS IDEA!
YESSIR!
37B 33

-UDERZO-

THERE! NOW WE'LL SAY GOODBYE, WITH APOLOGIES FOR FEARING THE POWER OF YOUR SECRET WEAPON!
OH, ANYONE CAN MAKE A MISTAKE!

BUT NEVER MIND! WE CAME ALL THIS WAY FOR NOTHING, FORGETTING THAT WE'RE THE MR BIGS OF THE ENTIRE UNIVERSE ANYWAY!
YOU KNOW, HE'S RIGHT!
?!
38 A

WHAT... WHAT'S HAPPENING TO ME?
OH NO ... HE'S AN INFLATED VIOLET NOW! I NEVER EXPECTED THIS!

OH, WHY DID I EVER COME HERE? WHEN I WAS SO HAPPY AT HOME ON MY OWN STAR!
?
IT'S THE DELAYED EFFECT OF MY POTION WORKING ON HIS INFLATED IDEA OF HIMSELF! HE NEEDS A SHRINK!
AND TO THINK I THOUGHT YOU'D BREWED A DUD POTION, GETAFIX!
I THINK HE MAY HAVE STOPPED GROWING!
38 B

AND HOW AM I GOING TO GET INTO MY SPACE-SPHERE NOW?

NEVER FEAR! THE EFFECTS OF MY POTION AREN'T PERMANENT. YOU'LL SOON BE BACK TO NORMAL!
HE'S RIGHT! HE REALLY IS MR BIG NOW!
38 C
33

-UDERZO-

AND NIGHT FALLS ON THE VILLAGE WHERE SOME PEOPLE ARE GETTING NO SLEEP AT ALL ...

STOP FLYING ABOUT LIKE THAT! YOU MAKE MY HEAD GO ROUND AND ROUND!

AMUSING, REALLY ... LIKE MOTHS ATTRACTED TO A CANDLE FLAME!

39B
33

-UDERZO-

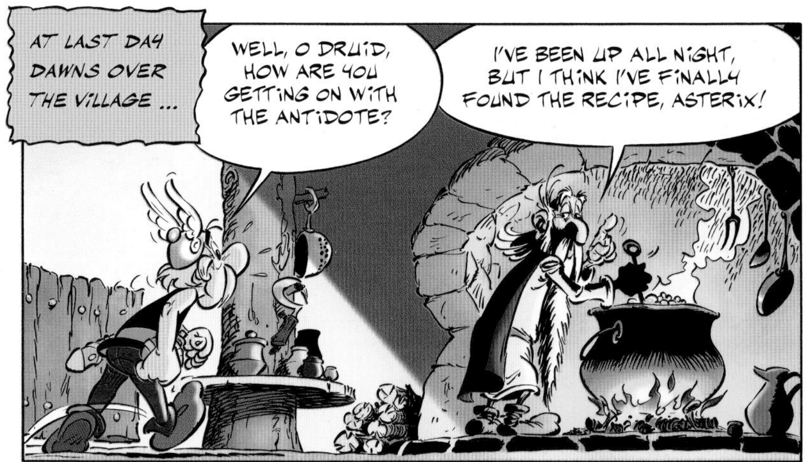
AT LAST DAY DAWNS OVER THE VILLAGE ...
WELL, O DRUID, HOW ARE YOU GETTING ON WITH THE ANTIDOTE?
I'VE BEEN UP ALL NIGHT, BUT I THINK I'VE FINALLY FOUND THE RECIPE, ASTERIX!

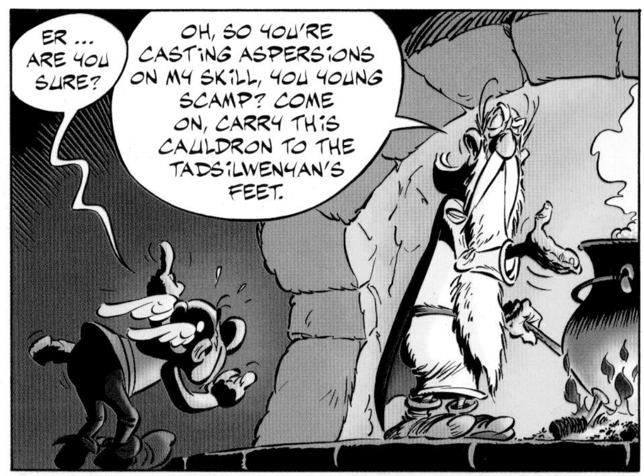
ER ... ARE YOU SURE?
OH, SO YOU'RE CASTING ASPERSIONS ON MY SKILL, YOU YOUNG SCAMP? COME ON, CARRY THIS CAULDRON TO THE TADSILWENYAN'S FEET.

HEY THERE, FRIEND! I'M BRINGING YOU A POTION WHICH WILL FIX EVERYTHING!

ER ... ARE YOU REALLY SURE THIS TIME?
OH NO! DON'T YOU START ON LIKE THAT TOO!
40A 33

CHEERS, TOON! AND DON'T OVER-INDULGE!

GULP!
I ONLY HOPE IT WORKS!

PSSSSCHHHH!
THERE WE ARE!
ER ... YES, BUT ...
40B 33

-UDERZO-

THANK YOU! I'D ALMOST GIVEN UP HOPE! YOU'RE A MIRACLE-WORKER, DRUID!
OH, IT WAS NOTHING!
BOING!

BUT ... BUT I'M THE WRONG COLOUR!

OH DEAR ... I MUST HAVE ADDED TOO MUCH INDELIBLE CUTTLEFISH INK!
YOU MEAN IT'S INDELIBLE TOO?

LET'S KEEP CALM! I'M SURE I CAN FIX THIS SOMEHOW!

I THINK YOU LOOK REALLY GOOD IN SUITS OF SOLEMN BLACK!
SNIFF!

SOON AFTERWARDS ...
HERE'S AN INFUSION OF CONCENTRATED PARMA VIOLETS WHICH WILL GET YOU REBORN IN THE PURPLE!
IS THAT A PROMISE?
41A
33

YOU MAY BE FEELING OFF COLOUR JUST NOW, AND I ADMIT I MADE A MISTAKE, BUT I'M ASKING YOU TO TRUST ME AGAIN, TOON!

IF I'VE GOT IT WRONG THIS TIME I PROMISE I'LL SHAVE OFF MY BEARD!
GLUG! GLUG!

GOODBYE, FRIENDS! THIS TIME I REALLY AM GOING BACK TO MY OWN STAR!
41B
33

I'M BACK IN THE PURPLE AGAIN!
GETAFIX PASSES WITH FLYING COLOURS ... HE CAN KEEP HIS BEARD!
THAT'LL TEACH ME NOT TO BE CURIOUS IN FUTURE! I NEVER WANT TO TASTE YOUR GAULISH POTIONS AGAIN!

UDERZO

AND I CAN WORK MIRACLES TOO! I'LL FIX IT FOR THE GAULS TO REMEMBER NOTHING ABOUT ME, THUS OBLITERATING ALL TRACES OF THIS GROTESQUE ADVENTURE!

WHAT ... WHAT'S THE TADSILWENYAN DOING?

HE'S CRAZY! HE'S GOING TO CRUSH US ALL!!!

42A 33

BROOOOOOFFFFFF!

CROAK?

42B 33

UDERZO

AND TO FINISH THE JOB, I'LL DO THE SAME ABOVE THE ROMAN CAMP ... NOW ... GOODBYE EARTH!
43A 33
WHAT A STRANGE SORT OF SMOG!
ESPECIALLY FOR THE YEAR 50 BC!
MY HUT!
?
WHAT A BURNING SHAME!
MY HUT AND MY TREE ARE BOTH BURNT DOWN!
?
?!
?!
TEEHEEHEE!
43B 33
UDERZO

THIS TIME YOU'VE GONE TOO FAR! YOU'LL HAVE TO REBUILD WHAT YOU'VE DESTROYED, UNDERSTAND?
IT WASN'T ME ANYWAY!
BUT WE NEVER DID A THING!
I DON'T WANT TO KNOW!
I CAN HELP YOU MAKE A TREE GROW VERY FAST!*
* SEE THE MANSIONS OF THE GODS
SOMETHING TELLS ME THERE'LL BE A GOOD CROP OF BOARS TODAY, ASTERIX!
AS USUAL, OBELIX!
WOOF!
SOON AFTERWARDS...
HERE'S WHAT WE NEED FOR THE BANQUET, VITALSTATISTIX!
YOU KNOW, IT SEEMS AGES SINCE WE HAD ONE, BOYS!
I WONDER HOW I MANAGED TO EAT SO MUCH OF MY STOCK WITHOUT NOTICING?
44A 33
AND SO, HAVING LOST ALL MEMORY OF THEIR LAST ADVENTURE, FOR ONCE THE INVINCIBLE GAULS OF THE VILLAGE HOLD A BANQUET UNDER THE STARRY SKY FOR NO SPECIAL REASON, JUST BECAUSE THEY'RE GLAD TO KNOW THAT THEIR LIVES AND INDEPENDENCE ARE SAFE FOR GOOD!
DOO AAH DIDDY DIDDY DUM DIDDY DOO!*
TZOING! TZOING!
LADIES AND GENTLEMEN, I RAISE MY ... OH, I NEVER SHOULD HAVE SAID HE COULD SING ...
YUMMY ... THIS IS GOOD!
SCRUNCH! SCRUNCH!
I DON'T KNOW WHY THIS SUDDENLY OCCURS TO ME, BUT DO YOU THINK THERE CAN BE LIFE ANYWHERE BUT ON EARTH?
WHO KNOWS, ASTERIX, WHO KNOWS?
CALM DOWN, GERIATRIX DEAR!
THE END
UDERZO 5-05
* WELL-KNOWN GAULISH TUNE

"In this book I would like to pay tribute to the great creations of Tadsilweny... sorry, I mean the great creations of Walt Disney who, famous and amazing druid that he was, allowed some of his colleagues, myself included, to fall into the cauldron of a potion of which he alone knew the magical secret."

Albert Uderzo

137